MARCH 2013

To ...

With love

Lulu.

x x x

Stir-fry

100 everyday recipes

First published in 2011
LOVE FOOD is an imprint of Parragon Books Ltd

Parragon
Queen Street House
4 Queen Street
Bath BA1 1HE, UK

ISBN: 978-1-4454-3046-1

Printed in Indonesia
Photography by Charlie Paul

Produced by Ivy Contract

Notes for the Reader

This book uses both metric and imperial measurements. Follow the same units of measurement throughout; do not mix metric and imperial. All spoon measurements are level: teaspoons are assumed to be 5 ml, and tablespoons are assumed to be 15 ml. Unless otherwise stated, milk is assumed to be full fat, eggs and individual vegetables are medium, and pepper is freshly ground black pepper.

The times given are an approximate guide only. Preparation times differ according to the techniques used by different people and the cooking times may also vary from those given. Optional ingredients, variations or serving suggestions have not been included in the calculations.

Recipes using raw or very lightly cooked eggs should be avoided by infants, the elderly, pregnant women, convalescents and anyone suffering from an illness. Pregnant and breastfeeding women are advised to avoid eating peanuts and peanut products. Sufferers from nut allergies should be aware that some of the ready-made ingredients used in the recipes in this book may contain nuts. Always check the packaging before use. Vegetarians should be aware that some of the ready-made ingredients used in the recipes in this book may contain animal products. Always check the packaging before use.

Stir-fry

introduction	4
soups & appetizers	6
meat & poultry	50
fish & seafood	100
rice & noodles	136
vegetarian	170
index	208

introduction

As you will soon see when you start cooking recipes from this book, buying a good wok is one of the best investments in kitchen equipment that you will ever make. This incredibly versatile pan can be used for soups, deep-frying, steaming and, most importantly, for stir-frying, the favourite cooking method of the people of Southeastern and Eastern Asia.

Wok cooking is ideal for anyone who is always on the go, because the dishes are nutritious, very quick and easy to prepare and cook, and absolutely delicious. Cooked rapidly over a high heat, vegetables retain their crisp texture and vibrant colour, so that the visual appeal of a stir-fried dish matches its taste, and meat, poultry, fish, tofu or nuts add the protein. Wonderful sauces, made in advance and then stirred in to heat through before serving, add a finishing touch to these sizzling and delicious dishes.

A traditional wok is made of steel, and when you get it home it will need a little preparation before use, known as 'seasoning'. First of all, scrub off the protective oiled coating in warm, soapy water, rinse well and let half dry. Next, stand the damp wok on a hob over low heat until it is completely dry. Drizzle in a little oil and wipe it round the inside with kitchen paper. Continue heating until the oil smokes and burns off, then repeat with another coating of oil. The wok will darken in colour and should never need scrubbing again, just wiping carefully.

You can prepare for stir-fry cooking in a wok by buying in a few store-cupboard ingredients. Items such as rice and a variety of noodles, peanut, sesame and vegetable oils, coconut milk, soy sauce, canned water chestnuts and straw mushrooms, fish sauce, curry pastes, spices and cornflour will get you started and all you'll need are the fresh ingredients to enable you to whip up a feast in moments.

Take to the wok and have fun stir-frying!

soups & appetizers

mushroom & noodle soup

ingredients

serves 4

½ cucumber
2 tbsp vegetable oil
2 spring onions, finely chopped
1 garlic clove, cut into
    thin strips
125 g/4½ oz flat or open-cap
    mushrooms, thinly sliced
600 ml/1 pint water
25 g/1 oz Chinese rice noodles
¾ tsp salt
1 tbsp soy sauce

method

1 Halve the cucumber lengthways. Scoop out the seeds using a teaspoon, then slice the flesh thinly.

2 Heat the oil in a large preheated wok. Add the spring onions and garlic and stir-fry for 30 seconds. Add the mushrooms and stir-fry for 2–3 minutes.

3 Stir in the water. Break the noodles into short lengths and add to the soup. Bring to the boil, stirring.

4 Add the cucumber slices, salt and soy sauce and simmer for 2–3 minutes.

5 Ladle the soup into warmed bowls, distributing the noodles and vegetables evenly.

chicken noodle soup

ingredients

serves 4–6

1 sheet dried egg noodles from
    a 250 g/9 oz packet
1 tbsp corn oil
4 skinless, boneless chicken
    thighs, diced
1 bunch of spring onions, sliced
2 garlic cloves, chopped
2-cm/³⁄₄-inch piece fresh ginger,
    finely chopped
850 ml/1¹⁄₂ pints chicken stock
175 ml/6 fl oz coconut milk
3 tsp Thai red curry paste
3 tbsp peanut butter
2 tbsp light soy sauce
salt and pepper
1 small red pepper, deseeded
    and chopped
55 g/2 oz frozen peas

method

1 Place the noodles in a shallow heatproof dish and soak
   in boiling water according to the packet directions.

2 Meanwhile, heat the oil in a preheated wok. Add
   the chicken and stir-fry for 5 minutes, or until lightly
   browned. Add the white part of the spring onions,
   the garlic and ginger and stir-fry for 2 minutes.

3 Add the stock, coconut milk, curry paste, peanut butter
   and soy sauce. Season to taste with salt and pepper.
   Bring to the boil, stirring constantly, then simmer for
   8 minutes, stirring occasionally. Add the pepper, peas
   and green spring onion tops and cook for a further
   2 minutes.

4 Drain the noodles, then add them to the wok and
   heat through. Spoon into warmed serving bowls and
   serve immediately.

thai-style seafood soup

ingredients

serves 4

1.25 litres/2¼ pints fish stock
1 lemon grass stem, split
   lengthways
pared rind of ½ lime or
   1 fresh kaffir lime leaf
2.5-cm/1-inch piece fresh
   ginger, sliced
¼ tsp chilli paste, or to taste
4–6 spring onions
200 g/7 oz large or medium
   raw prawns, peeled
salt
250 g/9 oz scallops (16–20)
2 tbsp coriander leaves
fresh red chilli rings, to garnish

method

1 Place the stock in a wok with the lemon grass, lime rind, ginger and chilli paste. Bring just to the boil, then reduce the heat and simmer, covered, for 10–15 minutes.

2 Cut the spring onions in half lengthways, then slice crossways very thinly. Cut the prawns almost in half lengthways, keeping the tails intact. Devein if necessary.

3 Pour the stock through a sieve, then return to the wok and bring to a simmer, with bubbles rising at the edges and the surface trembling. Add the spring onions and cook for 2–3 minutes. Taste and season with salt, if needed. Stir in a little more chilli paste if wished.

4 Add the scallops and prawns and poach for 1 minute, or until they turn opaque and the prawns curl.

5 Drop in the coriander leaves, then ladle the soup into bowls, dividing the shellfish evenly, and garnish with chilli rings.

duck with spring onion soup

ingredients

serves 4

2 duck breasts, skin on
2 tbsp Thai red curry paste
2 tbsp vegetable or peanut oil
bunch of spring onions, chopped
2 garlic cloves, crushed
5-cm/2-inch piece fresh
   ginger, grated
2 carrots, sliced thinly
1 red pepper, deseeded and cut
   into strips
1 litre/1¾ pints chicken stock
2 tbsp sweet chilli sauce
3–4 tbsp Thai soy sauce
400 g/14 oz canned straw
   mushrooms, drained

method

1 Slash the skin of the duck 3 or 4 times with a sharp knife and rub in the curry paste. Cook the duck breasts, skin side down, in a wok over high heat for 2–3 minutes. Turn over, reduce the heat and cook for a further 3–4 minutes, until cooked through. Lift out and slice thickly. Set aside and keep warm.

2 Meanwhile, heat the oil in a wok and stir-fry half the spring onions, the garlic, ginger, carrots and red pepper for 2–3 minutes. Pour in the stock and add the chilli sauce, soy sauce and mushrooms. Bring to the boil, reduce the heat and simmer for 4–5 minutes.

3 Ladle the soup into warmed bowls, top with the duck slices and garnish with the remaining spring onions. Serve immediately.

hot & sour pork soup with bamboo shoots

ingredients

serves 4

2 large shiitake mushrooms
1.25 litres/2¼ pints chicken stock
125 g/4½ oz pork tenderloin, thinly
    sliced into narrow shreds
25 g/1 oz canned sliced bamboo
    shoots, drained
100 g/3½ oz firm tofu, cut into
    1-cm/½-inch cubes
1 tbsp Chinese rice wine or
    dry sherry
2 tsp light soy sauce
1 tbsp rice vinegar
¼ tsp freshly ground white pepper,
    or more to taste
2 spring onions, some green
    included, thinly sliced
    diagonally, to garnish
few drops sesame oil, to garnish

method

1 Remove the hard stalks from the mushrooms and slice the caps very thinly. Cut the slices in half.

2 Bring the stock to a rolling boil in a large wok. Reduce the heat, add the mushrooms and let the stock simmer for 5 minutes. Add the pork, bamboo shoots and tofu, and simmer for a further 5 minutes. Add the rice wine, soy sauce, vinegar and white pepper, and simmer for 1 minute.

3 Ladle into soup bowls and sprinkle with the spring onions and a few drops of sesame oil.

kara-age chicken

ingredients

serves 4

6 skinless, boneless chicken thighs,
    about 100 g/3½ oz each
4 tbsp shoyu (Japanese soy sauce)
4 tbsp mirin
2 tsp finely grated fresh ginger
2 garlic cloves, crushed
oil, for deep-frying
70 g/2½ oz potato flour
    or cornflour
pinch of salt
lemon wedges, to serve

method

1 Cut the chicken into large cubes and put in a bowl.
Add the soy sauce, mirin, ginger and garlic and turn the
chicken to coat well. Cover with clingfilm and marinate
in a cool place for 20 minutes.

2 Preheat a wok, then fill one-third full with oil, or use
a deep-fryer. Heat the oil to 180–190°C/350–375°F,
or until a cube of bread browns in 30 seconds.

3 Meanwhile, mix the potato flour with the salt in a bowl.
Lift the chicken out of the marinade and shake off any
excess. Drop it into the potato flour and coat well, then
shake off any excess.

4 Add the chicken to the oil, in batches, and cook for
6 minutes, or until crisp and brown. Remove, drain
on kitchen paper and keep hot while you cook the
remaining chicken.

5 Serve with lemon wedges.

spicy beef & mushroom wontons

ingredients

makes 12–15

12–15 square wonton wrappers
groundnut oil, for deep-frying

filling

125 g/4 oz lean sirloin or rump
    steak, minced
1 spring onion, green part
    included, finely chopped
2 button mushrooms, finely
    chopped
1 small garlic clove, finely chopped
½ tsp finely chopped fresh ginger
½ tsp soy sauce
¼ tsp salt
¼ tsp freshly ground white pepper
⅛ tsp Chinese five-spice seasoning
½ tsp cornflour
1 egg, beaten

soy-ginger-dipping sauce

3 tbs soy sauce
2 tbsp very finely chopped
    fresh ginger

method

1 To make the filling, combine the minced steak, spring onion, mushrooms, garlic and ginger in a bowl. Mix the soy sauce, salt, pepper, five-spice seasoning and cornflour to a thin paste. Add the paste to the beef mixture, then stir in half the beaten egg (use the remainder in another recipe). Stir until very well mixed.

2 Separate the wonton squares and place on a tray, rotating them so one corner is facing towards you. Cover with a clean damp tea towel to prevent cracking. Working with one square at a time, place a slightly rounded teaspoon of filling in the bottom corner 1 cm/½ inch away from the point. Fold the point over the filling, then roll up two thirds of the wrapper, leaving a point at the top. Moisten the right- and left-hand corners with a dab of water. Fold one corner over the other and press lightly to seal into a bishop's mitre shape. Continue until all the wontons are filled.

3 To make the dipping sauce combine the soy sauce and ginger in a small bowl and leave to stand for 15 minutes. Heat a large wok over a high heat. Pour in the oil and heat to 180°C/350°F or until a cube of bread browns in 30 seconds. Deep-fry the wontons for 4–5 minutes until golden brown. Remove and drain on crumpled kitchen paper. Serve with the dipping sauce.

fried lamb balls with spring onion sauce

ingredients

makes 36

450 g minced lamb
1 garlic clove, finely chopped
1 tsp finely chopped fresh ginger
1½ tbsp soy sauce
1 tsp Chinese rice wine or
    dry sherry
½ tsp salt
½ tsp sugar
½ tsp freshly ground white pepper
½ tbsp cornflour
1 egg, beaten
groundnut oil, for frying
snipped garlic chives, to garnish
shredded Chinese leaves, to serve

spring onion sauce

4 tbsp chopped spring onions
4 tbsp finely chopped fresh ginger
2 tbsp light soy sauce
1 tsp rice vinegar
4 tbsp rapeseed oil

method

1 Combine the lamb, garlic and ginger in a bowl. Mix the soy sauce, wine, salt, sugar, pepper, and cornflour to a thin paste. Add the paste to the lamb mixture, then stir in the beaten egg. Stir with a fork until very well mixed. Pinch off small pieces of mixture and roll between your palms to form balls the size of a large marble.

2 Heat a wok over a high heat, add the oil and when it is almost smoking add the balls. Fry the balls in batches for 3 minutes, turning half-way through. Drain on crumpled kitchen paper.

3 To make the dipping sauce combine the ingredients in a bowl and whisk very thoroughly until well blended.

4 Arrange a bed of shredded Chinese leaves on a serving platter. Arrange the lamb balls on top, and sprinkle with garlic chives. Divide the dipping sauce between two small bowls and serve with the lamb.

beef stir-fry

ingredients

serves 4

2 tbsp vegetable or peanut oil
2 medium red onions, sliced thinly
2 garlic cloves, chopped
2.5-cm/1-inch piece ginger,
    cut into thin sticks
2 x 115-g/4-oz beef fillets,
    sliced thinly
1 green pepper, deseeded
    and sliced
150 g/5½oz canned
    bamboo shoots
115 g/4 oz beansprouts
2 tbsp Thai magic paste
    (see below)
1 tbsp Thai red curry paste
handful of fresh coriander, chopped
few sprigs Thai basil
boiled rice, to serve

thai magic paste

whole bulb of garlic, peeled
bunch of fresh coriander
    leaves and roots, roughly
    chopped
55 g/2 oz white peppercorns

method

1 To make the Thai magic paste, pulse all the ingredients briefly in a blender or food processor to form a thick paste, or pound with a pestle until well mixed. Store in the refrigerator for 3–4 days or freeze in small amounts.

2 Heat the oil in a wok and stir-fry the onions, garlic and ginger for 1 minute.

3 Add the beef strips and stir-fry over high heat until browned all over.

4 Add the vegetables and the magic and curry pastes and cook for 2–3 minutes until blended and cooked.

5 Stir in the coriander and basil and serve immediately with rice.

variation

You can replace the green peppers with mangetout and add water chestnuts for a tasty variation to this recipe.

crispy pork dumplings

ingredients

makes 4

350 g/12 oz ground pork
2 tbsp finely chopped fresh
     coriander
1 garlic clove, crushed
1 fresh green chilli, deseeded
     and chopped
3 tbsp cornflour
1 egg white
½ tsp salt
16 wonton skins
1 tbsp water
vegetable or peanut oil,
     for cooking
chilli sauce, to serve

method

1 Put the pork in a bowl and beat in the coriander, garlic, chilli, 1 tablespoon of the cornflour, the egg white and salt. Beat together to a thick, smooth texture. With damp hands shape into 16 equal portions and roll into balls.

2 Put a pork ball in the centre of each wonton skin. Make a paste by mixing the remaining cornflour with 1 tablespoon of water. Brush the edges of the skins with the cornflour paste and gather them up around the filling to make half into small, sacklike parcels, and the rest into triangular shapes.

3 Arrange the dumplings in a single layer (in batches if need be) in the top of a steamer and cook over boiling water for 10–15 minutes, until the meat is cooked through.

4 Heat the oil in a wok and carefully drop the parcels into it. Deep-fry for 2–3 minutes, until golden brown and crisp. Drain on kitchen paper.

5 Serve hot with chilli sauce.

soft-wrapped pork & prawn rolls

ingredients

makes 20

115 g/4 oz firm tofu
3 tbsp vegetable or peanut oil
1 tsp finely chopped garlic
55 g/2 oz lean pork, shredded
115 g/4 oz raw prawns, peeled
    and deveined
½ small carrot, cut into short
    thin sticks
55 g/2 oz fresh or canned bamboo
    shoots, rinsed and shredded
    (if using fresh shoots, boil in
    water first for 30 minutes)
115 g/4 oz very finely sliced
    cabbage
55 g/2 oz mangetout, julienned
1-egg omelette, shredded
1 tsp salt
1 tsp light soy sauce
1 tsp Shaoxing rice wine
pinch of white pepper
20 soft spring roll skins
chilli bean sauce, to serve

method

1 Slice the tofu into thin slices horizontally and cook in 1 tablespoon of the oil until it turns golden brown. Cut into thin strips and set aside.

2 In a preheated wok, heat the remaining oil and stir-fry the garlic until fragrant. Add the pork and stir for about 1 minute, then add the prawns and stir for a further minute.

3 One by one, stirring well after each addition, add the carrot, bamboo shoots, cabbage, mangetout, tofu and finally, the shredded omelette.

4 Season with the salt, light soy sauce, Shaoxing rice wine and pepper. Stir for a further minute, then turn out into a serving dish.

5 To assemble each roll, smear a skin with a little chilli bean sauce and place a heaped teaspoon of the filling towards the bottom of the circle. Roll up the bottom edge to secure the filling, turn in the sides, and continue to roll up gently. Serve with chilli bean sauce on the side.

spring rolls

ingredients
makes 20–25

6 dried Chinese mushrooms,
    soaked in warm water
    for 20 minutes
1 tbsp vegetable or peanut oil
225 g/8 oz minced pork
1 tsp dark soy sauce
100 g/3½ oz fresh or canned
    bamboo shoots, rinsed and
    julienned (if using fresh
    shoots, boil in water first for
    30 minutes)
pinch of salt
100 g/3½ oz raw prawns, peeled,
    deveined and chopped
225 g/8 oz beansprouts, trimmed
    and roughly chopped
1 tbsp finely chopped spring
    onions
25 spring roll skins
1 egg white, lightly beaten
vegetable or peanut oil,
    for deep-frying

method

1 Squeeze out any excess water from the mushrooms and finely slice, discarding any tough stems.

2 In a preheated wok, heat the tablespoon of oil and stir-fry the pork until it changes colour. Add the dark soy sauce, bamboo shoots, mushrooms and a little salt. Stir over high heat for 3 minutes.

3 Add the prawns and cook for 2 minutes, then add the beansprouts and cook for a further minute. Remove from the heat and stir in the spring onion. Set aside to cool.

4 Place a tablespoon of the mixture towards the bottom of a skin. Roll once to secure the filling, then fold in the sides to create a 10-cm/4-inch piece and continue to roll up. Seal with egg white.

5 Heat enough oil for deep-frying in a wok or deep-fat fryer until it reaches 180–190°C/350–375°F, or until a cube of bread browns in 30 seconds. Without overcrowding the wok, fry the rolls for about 5 minutes until golden brown and crispy.

crispy wrapped prawns

ingredients

makes 4

16 large, unpeeled cooked prawns
juice of 1 lime
4 tbsp chilli sauce
16 wonton skins
vegetable or peanut oil,
    for deep-frying
plum sauce, to serve

method

1 Remove the heads and shell the prawns, but leave the tails intact. Place them in a non-metallic bowl, add the lime juice and toss lightly to coat. Set aside in a cool place for 30 minutes.

2 Spread a little chilli sauce over a wonton skin. Place a prawn diagonally across it, leaving the tail protruding. Fold the bottom corner of the skin over the prawn, fold the next corner up over the head, and then roll the prawn up in the skin so that the body is encased, but the tail is exposed. Repeat with the remaining skins, chilli sauce and prawns.

3 Heat the oil in a wok and deep-fry the prawns, in batches, until crisp and browned. Serve hot with plum sauce for dipping.

prawn toasts

ingredients

makes 16

100 g/3½ oz raw prawns, peeled
    and deveined
2 egg whites
2 tbsp cornflour
½ tsp sugar
pinch of salt
2 tbsp finely chopped coriander
    leaves
2 slices day-old white bread
vegetable or peanut oil,
    for deep-frying

method

1 Pound the prawns to a pulp in a pestle and mortar
    or with the base of a cleaver.

2 Mix the prawns with one of the egg whites and
    1 tablespoon of the cornflour. Add the sugar and salt
    and stir in the chopped coriander. Mix the remaining
    egg white with the remaining cornflour.

3 Remove the crusts from the bread and cut each slice
    into 8 triangles. Brush the top of each piece with the
    egg white and cornflour mixture, then add 1 teaspoon
    of the prawn mixture. Smooth the top.

4 Heat enough oil for deep-frying in a wok until it
    reaches 180–190°C/350–375°F, or until a cube of bread
    browns in 30 seconds. Without overcrowding the wok,
    cook the toasts prawn-side up for about 2 minutes.
    Turn and cook for a further 2 minutes, or until
    beginning to turn golden brown.

5 Drain and serve warm.

crisp sesame prawns

ingredients

makes 4

115 g/4 oz self-raising flour
3 tbsp sesame seeds, toasted
   or dry-fried
1 tsp Thai red curry paste
1 tbsp fish sauce
150 ml/5 fl oz water
vegetable or peanut oil,
   for deep-frying
20 large, uncooked prawns,
   peeled with tails intact
chilli sauce, for dipping

method

1 Combine the flour and sesame seeds in a bowl. Stir the curry paste, fish sauce and water together in a jug until mixed. Gradually pour the liquid into the flour, stirring constantly, to make a thick batter.

2 Heat the oil for deep-frying in a wok. Holding the prawns by their tails, dip them into the batter, one at a time, then carefully drop into the hot oil. Cook for 2–3 minutes, until crisp and brown. Drain on kitchen paper.

3 Serve immediately with chilli sauce.

crab parcels

ingredients

makes 4

350 g/12 oz canned white
   crabmeat, drained
1 fresh red chilli, deseeded
   and chopped
4 spring onions, sliced finely
1 tbsp Thai red curry paste
juice of ½ lime
½ tsp salt
20 wonton skins
oil for cooking

dip
55 g/2 oz caster sugar
2 tbsp water
2 tbsp rice wine vinegar
3 pieces preserved ginger, sliced
1 tbsp ginger syrup from the jar

method

1 Put the crabmeat into a bowl and add the chilli, spring
   onions and curry paste. Stir together with the lime juice
   and salt.

2 Put the wonton skins in a pile and put 1 portion of the
   crabmeat in the centre of the top skin. Brush the edges
   with a little water and roll up the edges to make a small
   cigar-shaped parcel. Continue to make parcels with the
   skins – you need at least 20.

3 Heat the oil in a wok and cook the parcels, a few at
   a time, until golden brown. Drain on kitchen paper.

4 Put all the ingredients for the dip in a small pan and
   heat gently until the sugar has melted. Serve warm
   with the crab parcels.

vegetarian spring rolls

ingredients

makes 18–20

6 dried Chinese mushrooms,
    soaked in warm water for
    20 minutes
55 g/2 oz beanthread noodles,
    soaked in warm water for
    20 minutes
2 tbsp vegetable or peanut oil
1 tbsp finely chopped
    fresh ginger
100 g/3½ oz carrot, julienned
100 g/3½ oz finely shredded
    cabbage
1 tbsp finely sliced spring onion
1 tbsp light soy sauce
85 g/3 oz soft tofu,
    cut into small cubes
½ tsp salt
pinch of white pepper
pinch of sugar
20 spring roll skins
1 egg white, lightly beaten
vegetable or peanut oil,
    for deep-frying
soy sauce, for dipping

method

1 Squeeze out any excess water from the mushrooms
and finely chop, discarding any tough stems. Drain the
beanthread noodles and roughly chop.

2 In a preheated wok, heat the oil, then toss in the ginger
and cook until fragrant. Add the mushrooms and stir
for about 2 minutes. Add the carrot, cabbage and
spring onion and stir-fry for 1 minute. Add the
beanthread noodles and light soy sauce and stir-fry for
1 minute. Add the tofu and cook for a further minute.
Season with the salt, pepper and sugar and mix well.
Continue cooking for 1–2 minutes, or until the carrot
is soft. Remove from the heat and set aside to cool.

3 Place a scant tablespoon of the mixture towards the
bottom of a skin. Roll once to secure the filling, then
fold in the sides to create a 10-cm/4-inch piece and
continue to roll up. Seal with egg white.

4 Heat enough oil for deep-frying in a wok or deep-fat
fryer until it reaches 180–190°C/350–375°F, or until
a cube of bread browns in 30 seconds. Without
overcrowding the wok, cook the rolls for about
5 minutes, or until golden brown and crispy.

5 Serve with a good soy sauce for dipping.

vegetable parcels

ingredients

serves 4

2 tbsp vegetable or peanut oil
225 g/8 oz potatoes, diced and
    boiled for 5 minutes
2 garlic cloves, crushed
1 onion, chopped
2 tbsp Thai green curry paste
55 g/2 oz frozen peas, thawed
juice of 1 lime
½ tsp salt
16 x 10-cm/4-inch square
    egg roll skins
1 egg, beaten
vegetable or peanut oil,
    for deep-frying
sweet chilli sauce or Thai soy sauce,
    to serve

method

1 Heat the oil in a wok and stir-fry the potatoes, garlic, onion and curry paste until lightly browned. Stir in the peas, lime juice, and salt and stir-fry for 1–2 minutes. Remove from the heat.

2 Brush 1 egg roll skin with egg. Put a small spoonful of the potato mixture in the centre and fold up the edges to enclose the filling and make a purse-shaped parcel. Press the skin tightly together to seal the parcel. Repeat with the remaining skins and filling to make 16 small parcels.

3 Heat the oil for deep-frying in a wok. Add the vegetable parcels, in batches, and deep-fry for 3–4 minutes, until golden brown. Drain on kitchen paper and keep the parcels warm while you cook the remaining parcels.

4 Serve hot with a bowl of chilli sauce or soy sauce for dipping.

wontons

ingredients

serves 4

filling

2 tbsp vegetable or peanut oil
6 spring onions, chopped
125 g/4½ oz mushrooms,
    chopped
55 g/2 oz fine green beans,
    chopped
55 g/2 oz sweetcorn kernels,
    drained if canned
1 egg, beaten
3 tbsp Thai soy sauce
1 tbsp jaggery or soft light
    brown sugar
½ tsp salt

wontons

24 wonton skins
1 egg, beaten
vegetable or peanut oil,
    for deep-frying
plum or chilli sauce, to serve

method

1 To make the filling, heat the oil in a preheated wok and stir-fry the spring onions, mushrooms and beans for 1–2 minutes, until softened. Add the sweetcorn, stir well to mix and then push the vegetables to the side.

2 Pour in the egg. Stir until lightly set before incorporating the vegetables and adding the soy sauce, sugar and salt. Remove the wok from the heat.

3 Place the wonton skins in a pile on a work surface. Put a teaspoonful of the filling in the centre of the top skin. Brush the edges with beaten egg and fold in half diagonally to make a small triangular parcel. Repeat with the remaining skins and filling.

4 Heat the oil for deep-frying in a wok. Add the parcels, in batches, and deep-fry for 3–4 minutes, until golden brown. Remove from the wok with a slotted spoon and drain on kitchen paper. Keep warm while you cook the remaining wontons.

5 Serve hot with plum or chilli sauce.

crispy seaweed

ingredients

serves 4

1 kg/2 lb 4 oz pak choi
850 ml/1½ pints peanut oil
1 tsp salt
1 tbsp caster sugar
85 g/3 oz toasted pine nuts

method

1 Rinse the pak choi leaves under cold running water, then pat dry thoroughly with kitchen paper.

2 Discarding any tough outer leaves, roll each pak choi leaf up, then slice thinly so that the leaves are finely shredded. Alternatively, use a food processor to shred the pak choi.

3 Heat the peanut oil in a large preheated wok. Carefully add the shredded pak choi and cook for 30 seconds, or until it shrivels up and becomes crispy. (You will probably need to do this in several batches.) Remove the pak choi from the wok with a slotted spoon and drain thoroughly on kitchen paper.

4 Transfer to a large bowl, toss with the salt, sugar and toasted pine nuts, and serve.

tempura

ingredients

serves 4

150 g/5¹/₂ oz packet
    tempura mix
4 shiitake mushrooms
4 fresh asparagus spears
4 slices sweet potato
1 red pepper, deseeded and
    cut into strips
4 onion slices, cut widthways
    into rings
oil, for deep-frying

dipping sauce

2 tsp mirin
1 tbsp shoyu (Japanese soy sauce)
pinch of dashi granules, dissolved
    in 2 tbsp boiling water

method

1 To make the dipping sauce, mix the ingredients together in a small dipping dish.

2 Mix the tempura with water according to the packet instructions. Don't try to make the batter smooth – it should be a little lumpy. Drop the vegetables into the batter.

3 Preheat a wok, then fill two-thirds full with oil, or use a deep-fryer. Heat the oil to 180–190°C/350–375°F, or until a cube of bread browns in 30 seconds.

4 Lift 2–3 pieces of tempura out of the batter, add to the oil and cook for 2–3 minutes, or until the batter is a light golden colour. Remove, drain on kitchen paper and keep hot while you cook the remaining tempura pieces.

5 Serve with the dipping sauce.

meat & poultry

beef with onions & broccoli

ingredients

serves 4

2 tbsp vegetable or peanut oil

2 tbsp Thai green curry paste

2 x 175-g/6-oz sirloin steaks,
   sliced thinly

2 onions, sliced

6 spring onions, chopped

2 shallots, chopped finely

225 g/8 oz head of broccoli,
   cut into florets

400 ml/14 fl oz coconut milk

3 kaffir lime leaves, chopped
   roughly

4 tbsp chopped fresh coriander

few Thai basil leaves

method

1 Heat the oil in a wok and stir-fry the curry paste for
   1–2 minutes. Add the meat, in batches if necessary,
   and stir-fry until starting to brown.

2 Add the onions, spring onions and shallots, and
   stir-fry for 2–3 minutes. Add the broccoli and stir-fry
   for 2–3 minutes.

3 Pour in the coconut milk, add the lime leaves and
   bring to the boil. Simmer gently for 8–10 minutes, until
   the meat is tender. Stir in the coriander and basil and
   serve immediately.

beef chop suey

ingredients

serves 4

450 g/1 lb ribeye or sirloin steak,
    finely sliced
1 head of broccoli, cut into
    small florets
2 tbsp vegetable or peanut oil
1 onion, finely sliced
2 celery stalks, finely sliced
    diagonally
225 g/8 oz mangetout, sliced
    in half lengthways
55 g/2 oz fresh or canned bamboo
    shoots, rinsed and julienned
    (if using fresh shoots, boil in
    water first for 30 minutes)
8 water chestnuts, finely sliced
225 g/8 oz finely sliced
    mushrooms
1 tbsp oyster sauce
1 tsp salt
freshly cooked rice, to serve

marinade

1 tbsp Shaoxing rice wine
pinch of white pepper
pinch of salt
1 tbsp light soy sauce
½ tsp sesame oil

method

1 Combine all the marinade ingredients in a bowl and
  marinate the beef for at least 20 minutes. Blanch the
  broccoli in a large pan of boiling water for 30 seconds.
  Drain and set aside.

2 In a preheated wok, heat 1 tablespoon of the oil and
  stir-fry the beef until the colour has changed. Remove
  and set aside.

3 In the clean wok, heat the remaining oil and stir-fry
  the onion for 1 minute. Add the celery and broccoli
  and cook for 2 minutes. Add the mangetout, bamboo
  shoots, chestnuts and mushrooms and cook for
  1 minute. Add the beef, then season with the oyster
  sauce and salt and serve with freshly cooked rice.

spicy beef with potato

ingredients

serves 4

450 g/1 lb beef fillet
2 tbsp Thai soy sauce
2 tbsp fish sauce
2 tbsp vegetable or peanut oil
3–4 coriander roots, chopped
1 tbsp crushed black peppercorns
2 garlic cloves, chopped
1 tbsp jaggery or soft light
  brown sugar
350 g/12 oz potatoes, diced
150 ml/5 fl oz water
bunch of spring onions, chopped
225 g/8 oz baby spinach leaves
cooked rice or noodles, to serve

method

1 Cut the beef into thick slices and place in a shallow dish. Put the soy sauce, fish sauce, 1 tablespoon of the oil, the coriander roots, peppercorns, garlic and sugar in a food processor and process to a thick paste. Scrape the paste into the dish and toss the beef to coat. Cover with clingfilm and set aside to marinate in the refrigerator for at least 3 hours, and preferably overnight.

2 Heat the remaining oil in a wok. Lift the beef out of the marinade, reserving the marinade, and cook for 3–4 minutes on each side, until browned. Add the reserved marinade and the potatoes with the measured water and gradually bring to the boil. Simmer for 6–8 minutes, or until the potatoes are tender.

3 Add the spring onions and spinach. Cook gently until the greens have wilted. Serve immediately with rice or noodles.

stir-fried beef with broccoli & ginger

ingredients

serves 4–6

350 g/12 oz tenderloin steak,
   cut into thin strips
175 g/6 oz broccoli florets
2 tbsp vegetable or peanut oil
1 garlic clove, finely chopped
1 tsp finely chopped
   fresh ginger
1 small onion, finely sliced
1 tsp salt
1 tsp light soy sauce

marinade

1 tbsp light soy sauce
1 tsp sesame oil
1 tsp Shaoxing rice wine
1 tsp sugar
pinch of white pepper

method

1 Combine the marinade ingredients in a bowl, then
   mix in the beef. Cover and stand for 1 hour, basting
   occasionally. Blanch the broccoli in a large pan of
   boiling water for 30 seconds. Drain and set aside.

2 In a preheated wok, heat 1 tablespoon of the oil
   and stir-fry the garlic, ginger and onion for 1 minute.
   Add the broccoli and stir-fry for a further minute.
   Remove from the wok and set aside.

3 In the clean preheated wok, heat the remaining oil
   and stir-fry the beef until the colour has changed.
   Return the broccoli mixture to the wok with the salt
   and light soy sauce and stir until cooked through.
   Serve immediately.

ma po doufu

ingredients

serves 4

450 g/1 lb tofu
2 tbsp vegetable or peanut oil
1 tsp Sichuan peppers
100 g/3½ oz minced beef
2 tbsp chilli bean sauce
1 tsp fermented black beans,
    rinsed and lightly mashed
100 ml/3½ fl oz hot chicken stock
pinch of sugar
1 tsp light soy sauce
pinch of salt
2 tbsp thinly sliced spring onion,
    cut on the diagonal

method

1 Cut the tofu into 2-cm/¾-inch cubes and arrange in a large pan. Pour over enough boiling water to cover and set aside.

2 In a preheated wok, heat the oil until almost smoking. Throw in the Sichuan peppers and stir until fragrant. Add the beef and stir-fry until brown and crispy.

3 Lower the heat and add the chilli bean sauce and black beans and stir for about 30 seconds, or until the oil is richly red.

4 Pour in the hot chicken stock and gently add the drained tofu. Season with the sugar, light soy sauce and salt. Simmer for about 5 minutes.

5 Finally, toss in the spring onion. Transfer into 1 large or 4 individual bowls and serve.

katsudon

ingredients

serves 4

4 tbsp plain flour
1 egg, lightly beaten
115 g/4 oz Tonkatsu (panko) breadcrumbs
4 pork chops, about 150 g/5½ oz each, bones removed
oil, for pan-frying
600 ml/1 pint dashi stock
4 tbsp shoyu (Japanese soy sauce)
2 tbsp mirin
1 onion, sliced
4 eggs
600 g/1 lb 5 oz cooked Japanese short-grain rice

method

1 Put the flour, egg and breadcrumbs separately into 3 shallow bowls large enough to fit a pork chop. Roll a rolling pin over each chop to thin it a little.

2 Dip each chop first in the flour, then in the egg and finally in the breadcrumbs to coat. Cover with clingfilm and chill in the refrigerator for 10 minutes, then dip again in the egg and the breadcrumbs.

3 Preheat a wok over high heat. Add oil to a depth of about 2 cm/¾ inch and heat until very hot. Add the chops, one at a time, reduce the heat to medium and cook for 4 minutes on each side, or until the pork is cooked through and the breadcrumbs are golden. Remove and slice.

4 Meanwhile, put the stock, soy sauce and mirin in a pan and bring to a simmer. Add the onion and simmer for 5 minutes. Beat the eggs in a bowl, then pour over the onions in the stock. Cover and cook for 1 minute.

5 Divide the rice between 4 bowls. Lay the pork slices on top, then ladle some of the egg, onion and stock over the pork and rice. Serve immediately.

pork stir-fry with cashews, lime & mint

ingredients

serves 2

280 g/10 oz pork fillet
1 tsp coriander seeds
½ tsp white peppercorns
¼ tsp salt
¼ tsp sugar
juice and finely grated rind
    of 1 lime
2 tbsp groundnut oil
1 tsp finely chopped fresh ginger
1 garlic clove, thinly sliced
3 spring onions, white and green
    parts separated, then halved
    lengthways and sliced into
    2-cm/¾-inch pieces
1 small green pepper, deseeded
    and thinly sliced
2 tbsp cashew nuts, roughly
    chopped
large pinch of salt
1 tbsp chicken stock
1 tsp Thai fish sauce
2 tbsp roughly chopped fresh mint,
    to garnish

method

1 Diagonally slice the pork across the grain into thin bite-sized pieces. Flatten with the back of a knife blade and spread out on a plate. Using a mortar and pestle, crush the coriander seeds, peppercorns, salt, sugar and lime rind together. Spread the mixture over both sides of the pork, pressing it in well. Leave to stand for 15 minutes.

2 Heat a wok over a high heat, then add 1 tablespoon of the oil. Stir-fry the pork for 2–3 minutes, until no longer pink. Transfer to a plate with the juices. Wipe the wok clean with kitchen paper.

3 Heat the wok over a medium–high heat, then add the remaining oil. Stir-fry the ginger and garlic for a few seconds. Add the white spring onion and green pepper, and stir-fry for 2 minutes. Add the cashew nuts and salt, then stir-fry for a further minute.

4 Increase the heat to high, then return the pork and juices to the wok. Add the stock, lime juice, fish sauce and the green spring onion. Stir-fry for 30 seconds to heat through, then sprinkle with the mint and serve.

pork, carrot & ginger stir-fry

ingredients

serves 2

250 g/9 oz pork fillet
2 tbsp groundnut oil
2 large garlic cloves, thinly sliced
1 fresh green chilli, deseeded and
    thinly sliced diagonally
6 carrots, cut into thin strips
50 g/1¾ oz fresh ginger, cut into
    thin strips
140 g/5 oz canned bamboo shoots,
    drained
1½ tsp Sichuan peppers, crushed
100 ml/3½ fl oz chicken stock
2 tbsp light soy sauce

marinade

2 tsp Chinese rice wine
    or dry sherry
2 tsp light soy sauce
½ tsp sugar
¼ tsp salt

method

1 Diagonally slice the pork across the grain very thinly,
   then cut into 4-cm/1½-inch lengths. Put in a bowl.
   Combine the marinade ingredients and pour over
   the pork. Leave to stand for 30 minutes.

2 Heat a wok over a medium heat, then add the oil.
   Stir-fry the garlic and chilli for 30 seconds, or until
   the garlic just starts to colour.

3 Add the pork and marinade, and increase the heat
   to high. Stir-fry for 1 minute, then add the carrots,
   ginger, bamboo shoots and Sichuan peppers. Stir-fry
   for a further minute, then pour in the stock and soy
   sauce. Stir-fry for 4–5 minutes, until the sauce has
   reduced slightly. Transfer to a warmed dish and
   serve immediately.

spicy sichuan pork

ingredients

serves 4

280 g/10 oz pork belly, thinly
    sliced
1 tbsp vegetable or peanut oil
1 tbsp chilli bean sauce
1 tbsp fermented black beans,
    rinsed and lightly mashed
1 tsp sweet red bean paste
    (optional)
1 green pepper, finely sliced
1 red pepper, finely sliced
1 tsp sugar
1 tsp dark soy sauce
pinch of white pepper
freshly cooked rice, to serve

method

1 If cooking the pork especially for this dish, bring a pan
of water to the boil and place the pork in the pan, then
cover and simmer for about 20 minutes, skimming
occasionally. Let the pork cool and rest before
slicing thinly.

2 In a preheated wok, heat the oil and stir-fry the pork
slices until they begin to shrink. Stir in the chilli bean
sauce, then add the black beans and the red bean
paste, if using. Finally, toss in the peppers and the
remaining ingredients and stir-fry for 2 minutes.
Serve with freshly cooked rice.

pork with peppers

ingredients

serves 4

1 tbsp vegetable or peanut oil
1 tbsp chilli oil
450 g/1 lb pork fillet, sliced thinly
2 tbsp green chilli sauce
6 spring onions, sliced
2.5-cm/1-inch piece fresh
    ginger, sliced thinly
1 red pepper, deseeded
    and sliced
1 yellow pepper, deseeded
    and sliced
1 orange pepper, deseeded
    and sliced
1 tbsp fish sauce
2 tbsp Thai soy sauce
juice of ½ lime
4 tbsp chopped fresh parsley
cooked flat rice noodles, to serve

method

1 Heat both the oils in a wok. Add the pork, in batches, and stir-fry until browned all over. Remove with a slotted spoon and set aside.

2 Add the chilli sauce, spring onions and ginger to the wok and stir-fry for 1–2 minutes. Add the peppers and stir-fry for 2–3 minutes.

3 Return the meat to the wok, stir well and add the fish sauce, soy sauce and lime juice. Cook for a further 1–2 minutes, then stir in the parsley and serve with flat rice noodles.

variation

Try this recipe with chicken instead of pork, it will make a delicious alternative.

spareribs in a sweet-&-sour sauce

ingredients

serves 4

450 g/1 lb spareribs, cut into
    bite-size pieces (you or your
    butcher can cut ribs into pieces
    with a cleaver)
vegetable or peanut oil,
    for deep-frying

marinade
2 tsp light soy sauce
½ tsp salt
pinch of white pepper

sweet-&-sour sauce
3 tbsp white rice vinegar
2 tbsp sugar
1 tbsp light soy sauce
1 tbsp tomato ketchup
1½ tbsp vegetable or peanut oil
1 green pepper, roughly chopped
1 small onion, roughly chopped
1 small carrot, finely sliced
½ tsp finely chopped garlic
½ tsp finely chopped ginger
100 g/3½ oz pineapple chunks

method

1 Combine the marinade ingredients in a bowl with
the pork and marinate for at least 20 minutes.

2 Heat enough oil for deep-frying in a wok or deep-fat
fryer until it reaches 180–190°C/350–375°F, or until
a cube of bread browns in 30 seconds. Deep-fry the
spareribs for 8 minutes. Drain and set aside.

3 To prepare the sauce, first mix together the vinegar,
sugar, light soy sauce and ketchup. Set aside.

4 In a preheated wok, heat 1 tablespoon of the oil and
stir-fry the pepper, onion and carrot for 2 minutes.
Remove and set aside.

5 In the clean preheated wok, heat the remaining
oil and stir-fry the garlic and ginger until fragrant.
Add the vinegar mixture. Bring back to the boil and
add the pineapple chunks. Finally add the spareribs
and the pepper, onion and carrot. Stir until warmed
through and serve immediately.

lamb & leek stir-fry

ingredients

serves 2

280 g/10 oz lamb neck fillet
1 garlic clove, finely chopped
2 tsp soy sauce
2 tsp Chinese rice wine or
    dry sherry
½ tsp sugar
¼ tsp salt
½ tbsp cornflour
3 tbsp chicken stock
2 tbsp groundnut oil
3 leeks, green part included, sliced
    into 4-cm/1½-inch pieces
1 tbsp chicken stock or water
pepper

method

1 Diagonally slice the lamb across the grain into thin bite-sized pieces. Flatten with the back of a knife blade and put in a bowl. Combine the garlic, soy sauce, rice wine, sugar and salt. Pour the mixture over the lamb. Leave to stand for 1 hour at room temperature, or overnight in the refrigerator.

2 Mix the cornflour to a thin paste with the chicken stock. Heat a wok over a high heat, then add 1 tablespoon of the oil. Add the lamb and stir-fry for 1 minute, then season to taste with pepper. Add the cornflour paste and stir-fry for a further minute. Remove from the wok and keep warm. Wipe the wok clean with kitchen paper.

3 Heat the wok over a high heat, then add the remaining oil. Add the leeks and chicken stock, and stir-fry for 2 minutes, until just cooked and still bright green and crisp. Return the lamb to the wok and stir-fry for 30 seconds. Transfer to a warmed serving dish and serve immediately.

chicken with cashew nuts

ingredients

serves 4–6

450 g/1 lb boneless chicken meat,
cut into bite-size pieces
3 tbsp light soy sauce
1 tsp Shaoxing rice wine
pinch of sugar
½ tsp salt
3 dried Chinese mushrooms,
soaked in warm water
for 20 minutes
2 tbsp vegetable or peanut oil
4 slices of fresh ginger
1 tsp finely chopped garlic
1 red pepper, cut into
2.5-cm/1-inch squares
85 g/3 oz cashew nuts, roasted

method

1 Marinate the chicken in 2 tablespoons of the light soy sauce, Shaoxing, sugar and salt for at least 20 minutes.

2 Squeeze any excess water from the mushrooms and slice finely, discarding any tough stems. Reserve the soaking water.

3 In a preheated wok, heat 1 tablespoon of the oil. Add the ginger and stir-fry until fragrant. Stir in the chicken and cook for 2 minutes, or until it begins to turn brown. Before the chicken is cooked through, remove and set aside.

4 In the clean wok, heat the remaining oil and stir-fry the garlic until fragrant. Add the mushrooms and red pepper and stir-fry for 1 minute. Add about 2 tablespoons of the mushroom soaking water and cook for about water has evaporated.

5 Return the chicken to the wok, then add the remaining light soy sauce and the cashew nuts and stir-fry for 2 minutes, or until the chicken is cooked through.

sweet-&-sour chicken

ingredients

serves 4–6

450 g/1 lb lean chicken meat, cubed
5 tbsp vegetable or peanut oil
½ tsp crushed garlic
½ tsp finely chopped fresh ginger
1 green pepper, roughly chopped
1 onion, roughly chopped
1 carrot, finely sliced
1 tsp sesame oil
1 tbsp finely chopped spring onion

marinade

2 tsp light soy sauce
1 tsp Shaoxing rice wine
pinch of white pepper
½ tsp salt
dash of sesame oil

sauce

8 tbsp rice vinegar
4 tbsp sugar
2 tsp light soy sauce
6 tbsp tomato ketchup

method

1 Place all the marinade ingredients in a bowl and marinate the chicken pieces for at least 20 minutes.

2 To prepare the sauce, heat the vinegar in a pan and add the sugar, light soy sauce and tomato ketchup. Stir to dissolve the sugar, then set aside.

3 In a preheated wok, heat 3 tablespoons of the oil and stir-fry the chicken until it starts to turn golden brown. Remove and set aside.

4 In the clean wok, heat the remaining oil and cook the garlic and ginger until fragrant. Add the vegetables and cook for 2 minutes. Add the chicken and cook for 1 minute. Finally add the sauce and sesame oil, then stir in the spring onion and serve.

gong bau chicken

ingredients

serves 4

2 boneless chicken breasts, with
   or without skin, cut into
   1-cm/½-inch cubes
1 tbsp vegetable or peanut oil
10 dried red chillies or more, to
   taste, snipped into 2 or 3 pieces
1 tsp Sichuan peppers
3 garlic cloves, finely sliced
2.5-cm/1-inch piece of fresh
   ginger, finely sliced
1 tbsp roughly chopped spring
   onion, white part only
85 g/3 oz peanuts, roasted

marinade

2 tsp light soy sauce
1 tsp Shaoxing rice wine
½ tsp sugar

sauce

1 tsp light soy sauce
1 tsp dark soy sauce
1 tsp black Chinese rice vinegar
a few drops of sesame oil
2 tbsp chicken stock
1 tsp sugar

method

1 Combine all the ingredients for the marinade in a
   bowl and marinate the chicken, covered, for at least
   20 minutes. Combine all the ingredients for the sauce
   and set aside.

2 In a preheated wok, heat the oil and stir-fry the chillies
   and peppers until crisp and fragrant. Toss in the chicken
   pieces. When they begin to turn white, add the garlic,
   ginger and spring onion. Stir-fry for about 5 minutes,
   or until the chicken is cooked.

3 Pour in the sauce, mix together thoroughly, then
   stir in the peanuts. Serve immediately.

peppered chicken stir-fry

ingredients

serves 4–6

4 tsp soy sauce

1 tbsp cornflour

1 tbsp Chinese rice wine
   or dry sherry

¼ tsp salt

350 g/12 oz skinless, boneless
   chicken breasts, cut into cubes

6 tbsp chicken stock

1 tbsp oyster sauce

4 tbsp groundnut oil

1 tsp finely chopped fresh ginger

1 large garlic clove, thinly sliced

4 spring onions, white and green
   parts separated, diagonally
   sliced into 2-cm/¾-inch pieces

½ tbsp white peppercorns, crushed

8 baby corn, halved diagonally

½ small red pepper, deseeded
   and thinly sliced

140 g/5 oz canned water
   chestnuts, drained

115 g/4 oz mangetout, halved
   diagonally

method

1 In a small bowl, combine half the soy sauce, the cornflour, rice wine and salt.

2 Put the chicken pieces in a shallow dish and pour over the soy sauce mixture, stirring to coat. Leave to stand for 15 minutes.

3 Mix the remaining soy sauce with the stock and oyster sauce, and set aside.

4 Heat a wok over a high heat, then add the oil. Add the chicken and stir-fry for 3 minutes, until no longer pink. Remove from the wok with a slotted spoon and drain on kitchen paper.

5 Reduce the heat slightly, then add the ginger, garlic, white spring onion and the crushed peppercorns, and stir for a few seconds. Add the baby corn, red pepper and water chestnuts. Stir-fry for 2 minutes, then return the chicken to the wok. Add the mangetout and the soy sauce mixture, and stir-fry for 1–2 minutes, until the sauce is thickened.

6 Sprinkle with the sliced green spring onion and cook for a few more seconds. Serve immediately.

ginger chicken with sesame seeds

ingredients

serves 4

500 g/1 lb 2 oz skinless, boneless
    chicken breasts, cut into strips
2 tbsp groundnut oil
1 leek, thinly sliced
1 head of broccoli, cut into
    small florets
2 carrots, thinly sliced
½ cauliflower, cut into small florets
1 tsp grated fresh ginger
5 tbsp white wine
2 tbsp sesame seeds
1 tbsp cornflour
1 tbsp water

marinade

4 tbsp soy sauce
4 tbsp water

method

1 Combine the marinade ingredients in a bowl. Add the chicken and toss to coat well. Cover with clingfilm and chill in the refrigerator for 1 hour.

2 Remove the chicken from the marinade with a slotted spoon. Heat a wok over a medium–high heat, then add the oil. Stir-fry the chicken and leek until the chicken is browned and the leek is beginning to soften. Stir in the remaining vegetables, the ginger and wine. Reduce the heat, cover and simmer for 5 minutes.

3 Place the sesame seeds on a baking tray under a hot grill. Stir them once to make sure they toast evenly. Set aside to cool.

4 In a small bowl, combine the cornflour with the water and mix until smooth. Gradually add the liquid to the wok, stirring constantly until thickened.

5 Sprinkle with the sesame seeds and serve immediately.

chicken with yellow curry sauce

ingredients

serves 4

spice paste
6 tbsp Thai yellow curry paste
150 ml/5 fl oz plain yogurt
400 ml/14 fl oz water
handful of fresh coriander,
    chopped
handful of fresh Thai basil
    leaves, shredded

stir-fry
2 tbsp vegetable or peanut oil
2 onions, cut into thin wedges
2 garlic cloves, chopped finely
2 skinless, boneless chicken
    breasts, cut into strips
175 g/6 oz baby corn cobs,
    halved lengthways
chopped fresh coriander and
    shredded fresh basil,
    to garnish

method

1 To make the spice paste, stir-fry the yellow curry paste
  in a wok for 2–3 minutes, then stir in the yogurt, water
  and herbs. Bring to the boil, then simmer for
  2–3 minutes.

2 Meanwhile, heat the oil in a wok and stir-fry the onions
  and garlic for 2–3 minutes. Add the chicken and baby
  corn cobs and stir-fry for 3–4 minutes, until the meat
  and corn are tender.

3 Stir in the spice paste and bring to the boil. Simmer for
  2–3 minutes, until heated through. Serve immediately,
  garnished with extra herbs if desired.

red chicken salad

ingredients

serves 4

4 boneless chicken breasts
2 tbsp Thai red curry paste
2 tbsp vegetable or peanut oil
1 head Chinese leaves, shredded
175 g/6 oz pak choi, torn into
    large pieces
1/2 savoy cabbage, shredded
2 shallots, chopped finely
2 garlic cloves, crushed
1 tbsp rice wine vinegar
2 tbsp sweet chilli sauce
2 tbsp Thai soy sauce

method

1 Slash the flesh of the chicken several times and rub
   the curry paste into each cut. Cover and chill overnight.

2 Cook in a wok over medium heat for 5–6 minutes,
   turning once or twice, until cooked through.
   Keep warm.

3 Heat 1 tablespoon of the oil in a wok and stir-fry
   the pak choi and cabbage until just wilted. Add the
   remaining oil, shallots and garlic, and stir-fry until just
   tender but not browned. Add the vinegar, chilli sauce
   and soy. Remove from the heat.

4 Arrange the leaves on 4 serving plates. Slice the
   chicken, arrange on the salad leaves and drizzle the
   hot dressing over. Serve immediately.

turkey teriyaki

ingredients

serves 4

450 g/1 lb turkey steaks,
cut into strips
3 tbsp groundnut oil
1 small yellow pepper, deseeded
and sliced into thin strips
8 spring onions, green part
included, diagonally sliced into
2.5-cm/1-inch pieces
freshly cooked plain rice, to serve

teriyaki glaze

5 tbsp shoyu (Japanese soy sauce)
5 tbsp mirin
2 tbsp clear honey
1 tsp finely chopped fresh ginger

method

1 Mix the glaze ingredients in a small saucepan over low–medium heat. Stir until the honey has melted, then remove from the heat and leave to cool.

2 Put the turkey in a large shallow dish. Pour over the glaze, turning the strips so they are well coated. Leave to marinate for 30 minutes at room temperature, or overnight in the refrigerator.

3 Using a slotted spoon, remove the turkey from the marinade, shaking off the excess liquid. Reserve the marinade.

4 Heat a wok over a medium–high heat, then add the oil. Add the turkey and stir-fry for 2 minutes. Add the yellow pepper and spring onions, and fry for 1 minute. Pour in the reserved marinade. Bring to the boil, then reduce the heat slightly and cook for 3–4 minutes, until the turkey is cooked through.

5 Transfer the turkey and vegetables to a warmed serving dish. Boil the liquid remaining in the wok until syrupy, then pour over the turkey. Serve immediately with rice.

turkey with bok choi & mushrooms

ingredients

serves 4

225 g/8 oz medium egg noodles
3 tbsp groundnut oil
1 large garlic clove, thinly sliced
2 tsp finely chopped fresh ginger
450 g/1 lb turkey steaks, cut into
thin strips
175 g/6 oz chestnut mushrooms,
thinly sliced
600 g/1 lb 5 oz bok choi, stalks cut
into 2.5-cm/1-inch squares
and leaves sliced into wide
ribbons
4 spring onions, green part
included, diagonally sliced into
2.5-cm/1-inch pieces
1 tbsp light soy sauce
2 tbsp chopped fresh coriander
salt and pepper

method

1 Cook the noodles in a saucepan of boiling water for
4 minutes, or according to the instructions on the
packet, until soft. Drain, rinse and drain again, then
leave to cool.

2 Heat a wok over a medium–high heat, then add the
oil. Stir-fry the garlic and ginger for a few seconds to
flavour the oil.

3 Add the turkey and stir-fry for 2 minutes, until no
longer pink. Add the mushrooms and bok choi stalks,
and stir-fry for 2 minutes. Add the bok choi leaves and
spring onions, and stir-fry for a further 2 minutes. Stir
in the noodles and soy sauce, and season to taste with
salt and pepper. Cook until the noodles are heated
through, then add the coriander. Serve immediately.

fruity duck stir-fry

ingredients

serves 4

4 skinless, boneless duck breasts
1 tsp Chinese five-spice
1 tbsp cornflour
1 tbsp chilli oil
225 g/8 oz baby onions, peeled
2 garlic cloves, crushed
100 g/3½ oz baby corn
175 g/6 oz canned pineapple
  chunks
6 spring onions, sliced
100 g/3½ oz fresh beansprouts
2 tbsp plum sauce

method

1 Using a sharp knife, cut the duck into thin slices.

2 Mix the Chinese five-spice and the cornflour. Toss the duck in the mixture until well coated.

3 Heat a wok over a high heat, then add the oil. Stir-fry the duck for 10 minutes, or until just beginning to crispen around the edges. Remove from the wok and set aside.

4 Add the onions and garlic to the wok and stir-fry for 5 minutes, or until softened. Add the baby corn and stir-fry for a further 5 minutes. Add the pineapple, spring onions and beansprouts and stir-fry for 3–4 minutes. Stir in the plum sauce.

5 Return the cooked duck to the wok and toss until well mixed. Transfer to warmed serving dishes and serve hot.

duck with mixed peppers

ingredients

serves 4

1 tbsp vegetable or peanut oil
2 duck breasts, skin on
1 onion, sliced
2 garlic cloves, chopped
1 red pepper, deseeded
    and chopped
1 green pepper, deseeded
    and chopped
1 yellow pepper, deseeded
    and chopped
4 tomatoes, peeled, deseeded
    and chopped
150 ml/5 fl oz stock
3 tbsp Thai soy sauce
boiled noodles, garnished with
    chopped onion, to serve

method

1 Heat the oil in a wok and cook the duck breasts over high heat until crisp and brown. Turn over and cook until cooked through. Lift out and keep warm.

2 Pour off any excess fat and stir-fry the onion and garlic for 2–3 minutes, until softened and lightly browned.

3 Add the peppers and stir-fry for 2–3 minutes, until tender. Add the tomatoes, stock and soy sauce, and simmer for 1–2 minutes. Transfer to a serving plate. Slice the duck thickly and arrange on top, spooning any sauce over it. Serve with noodles.

cantonese sweet & sour duck

ingredients

serves 6

2 boneless duck breasts, skin on,
    weighing about 550 g/
    1 lb 4 oz in total
½ tbsp soy sauce
2 tsp groundnut oil
salt and pepper
4-cm/1½-inch piece cucumber,
    peeled and sliced lengthways
    into matchsticks, to garnish

sauce

1 tbsp cornflour
125 ml/4 fl oz chicken stock
1½ tbsp soy sauce
1½ tbsp rice vinegar
2 tbsp sugar
1 tbsp tomato purée
1 tbsp orange juice
2 tsp groundnut oil
3 thin slices fresh ginger

method

1 Slice each duck breast into 3 pieces and put in a dish.
   Rub with salt and pepper and the half tablespoon of
   soy sauce.

2 Heat a wok over a medium–high heat, then add the oil.
   Fry the duck for 6 minutes, starting with the skin side
   down, and turning until brown and crisp on all sides.
   Using tongs, transfer to a plate and leave to rest in a
   warm place for 10 minutes. Discard the oil and wipe
   the wok clean. Slice the duck into 1-cm/½-inch strips.

3 To prepare the sauce, mix the cornflour to a smooth
   paste with 3 tablespoons of the stock. Combine the
   soy sauce, vinegar and sugar in a small bowl, stirring to
   dissolve the sugar. Add the tomato purée and orange
   juice, mixing well.

4 Heat the oil in the clean wok over a medium heat.
   Add the ginger slices and stir-fry for a few seconds
   to flavour the oil. Add the soy sauce mixture and the
   remaining stock, and bring to the boil. Reduce the
   heat slightly and add in the cornflour paste. Stir until
   starting to thicken, then add the duck slices. Simmer
   for 5 minutes, until the duck is cooked but slightly pink.

5 Remove the ginger slices and transfer the duck and
   sauce to a warmed serving dish. Garnish with the
   cucumber and serve immediately.

fish in coconut

ingredients

serves 4

2 tbsp vegetable or peanut oil
6 spring onions, chopped roughly
2.5-cm/1-inch piece fresh
  ginger, grated
2–3 tbsp Thai red curry paste
400 ml/14 fl oz coconut milk
150 ml/5 fl oz fish stock
4 kaffir lime leaves
1 lemon grass stalk, broken
  in half
350 g/12 oz white fish fillets,
  skinned and cut into chunks
225 g/8 oz squid rings and
  tentacles
225 g/8 oz large cooked
  peeled prawns
1 tbsp fish sauce
2 tbsp Thai soy sauce
4 tbsp chopped fresh
  Chinese chives
boiled jasmine rice with chopped
  fresh coriander, to serve

method

1 Heat the oil in a wok and stir-fry the spring onions and ginger for 1–2 minutes. Add the curry paste and stir-fry for 1–2 minutes.

2 Add the coconut milk, fish stock, lime leaves and lemon grass. Bring to the boil, then reduce the heat and simmer for 1 minute.

3 Add the fish, squid and prawns, and simmer for 2–3 minutes, until the fish is cooked. Add the fish and soy sauces and stir in the chives. Serve immediately with jasmine rice with fresh coriander stirred through it.

five-willow fish

ingredients

serves 4–6

1 whole sea bass or similar, weighing 450–675 g/ 1–1½ lb, gutted

2 tsp salt

6 tbsp vegetable or peanut oil

2 slices fresh ginger

2 garlic cloves, finely sliced

2 spring onions, roughly chopped

1 green pepper, thinly sliced

1 red pepper, thinly sliced

1 carrot, finely sliced

55 g/2 oz fresh or canned bamboo shoots, rinsed and thinly sliced (if using fresh shoots, boil in water first for 30 minutes)

2 tomatoes, peeled, deseeded and thinly sliced

1 tbsp Shaoxing rice wine

2 tbsp white rice vinegar

1 tbsp light soy sauce

1 tbsp sugar

method

1 Clean the fish and dry thoroughly. Score the fish on both sides with deep, diagonal cuts. Press ½ teaspoon of the salt into the skin.

2 In a preheated wok, heat 4 tablespoons of the oil and cook the fish for about 4 minutes on each side, or until the flesh is soft. Drain, then set aside and keep warm.

3 In the clean preheated wok, heat the remaining oil and stir-fry the ginger, garlic and spring onions until fragrant. Toss in the vegetables with the remaining salt and stir rapidly for 2–3 minutes. Add the remaining ingredients and mix well for 2–3 minutes. Pour the sauce over the fish and serve.

monkfish with lime & chilli sauce

ingredients

serves 4

4 x 115-g/4-oz
    monkfish fillets
25 g/1 oz rice flour
    or cornflour
6 tbsp vegetable or peanut oil
4 garlic cloves, crushed
2 large fresh red chillies,
    deseeded and sliced
2 tsp jaggery or soft light
    brown sugar
juice of 2 limes
grated rind of 1 lime
boiled rice, to serve

method

1 Toss the fish in the flour, shaking off any excess. Heat the oil in a wok and cook the fish on all sides until browned and cooked through, taking care when turning not to break it up.

2 Lift the fish out of the wok and keep warm. Add the garlic and chillies and stir-fry for 1–2 minutes, until they have softened.

3 Add the sugar, the lime juice and rind and 2–3 tablespoons of water and bring to the boil. Simmer gently for 1–2 minutes, then spoon the mixture over the fish. Serve immediately with rice.

fish curry

ingredients

serves 4

juice of 1 lime
4 tbsp fish sauce
2 tbsp Thai soy sauce
1 fresh red chilli, deseeded
    and chopped
350 g/12 oz monkfish fillet,
    cut into cubes
350 g/12 oz salmon fillets, skinned
    and cut into cubes
400 ml/14 fl oz coconut milk
3 kaffir lime leaves
1 tbsp Thai red curry paste
1 lemon grass stalk (white part
    only), chopped finely
2 cups jasmine rice, boiled
4 tbsp chopped fresh coriander

method

1 Combine the lime juice, half the fish sauce and the soy sauce in a shallow, non-metallic dish. Add the chilli and the fish, stir to coat, cover with clingfilm and chill for 1–2 hours, or overnight.

2 Bring the coconut milk to the boil in a wok and add the lime leaves, curry paste, the remaining fish sauce and the lemon grass. Simmer gently for 10–15 minutes.

3 Add the fish and the marinade and simmer for 4–5 minutes, until the fish is cooked. Serve hot with boiled rice with chopped coriander stirred through it.

mixed seafood curry

ingredients

serves 4

1 tbsp vegetable or peanut oil
3 shallots, chopped finely
2.5-cm/1-inch piece fresh
    galangal, peeled and sliced
    thinly
2 garlic cloves, chopped finely
400 ml/14 fl oz canned
    coconut milk
2 lemon grass stalks,
    snapped in half
4 tbsp fish sauce
2 tbsp chilli sauce
225 g/8 oz uncooked king
    prawns, peeled
225 g/8 oz baby squid, cleaned
    and sliced thickly
225 g/8 oz salmon fillet, skinned
    and cut into chunks
175 g/6 oz tuna steak,
    cut into chunks
225 g/8 oz fresh mussels,
    scrubbed and debearded
fresh Chinese chives, to garnish
boiled rice, to serve

method

1 Heat the oil in a large wok and stir-fry the shallots, galangal and garlic for 1–2 minutes, until they start to soften. Add the coconut milk, lemon grass, fish sauce and chilli sauce. Bring to the boil, reduce the heat, and simmer for 1–2 minutes.

2 Add the prepared prawns, squid, salmon and tuna, and simmer for 3–4 minutes, until the prawns have turned pink and the fish is cooked.

3 Add the mussels to the wok and cover with a lid. Simmer for 1–2 minutes, until they have opened. Discard any mussels that remain closed. Garnish with Chinese chives and serve immediately with rice.

steamed salmon with bok choi & asparagus

ingredients

serves 4

4 salmon steaks, about
    2.5 cm/1 inch thick
2 tsp finely chopped fresh ginger
2 tbsp Chinese rice wine or
    dry sherry
1 tbsp light soy sauce
½ tsp salt
8 asparagus spears, stalks chopped
    into 2 or 3 pieces, tips reserved
4 tbsp groundnut oil
3 heads bok choi, quartered
    lengthways
good squeeze of lime juice
2 tsp sesame oil
coarsely ground black pepper
freshly cooked plain rice, to serve

method

1 Place the salmon steaks in a single layer on a heatproof plate that will fit into a wok. Combine the ginger, wine, soy sauce and salt. Sprinkle this over the fish, rubbing it into the flesh, and leave to stand for 20 minutes, turning once.

2 Place a trivet in a wok with a lid, and add enough water to come halfway up the trivet. Bring to the boil, then place the plate of fish on the trivet and cover with a loose tent of foil. Adjust the heat so the water is only just boiling. Put the lid on the wok and steam for 10–15 minutes until the fish is opaque and just starting to flake. Meanwhile, heat a second wok over high heat, then add 2 tablespoons of the groundnut oil. Add the asparagus stalks and bok choi, and stir-fry for 4–5 minutes until just tender but still crisp. Splash with a good squeeze of lime juice and season with salt and pepper. Arrange on warm serving plates.

3 Carefully lift the salmon steaks from the wok and place on top of the vegetables. Heat the sesame oil and remaining groundnut oil until very hot. Add the asparagus tips and stir-fry for 20 seconds. Season with black pepper. Arrange the tips on top of the fish and pour the hot oil over the top. Serve at once with rice.

salmon & scallops with coriander & lime

ingredients

serves 4

6 tbsp groundnut oil
280 g/10 oz salmon steak,
    skinned and cut into
    2.5-cm/1-inch chunks
225 g/8 oz scallops
3 carrots, thinly sliced
2 celery stalks, cut into
    2.5-cm/1-inch pieces
2 yellow peppers, deseeded and
    thinly sliced
175 g/6 oz oyster mushrooms,
    thinly sliced
1 garlic clove, crushed
6 tbsp chopped fresh coriander
3 shallots, thinly sliced
juice of 2 limes
1 tsp lime zest
1 tsp dried red pepper flakes
3 tbsp dry sherry
3 tbsp soy sauce

method

1 Heat a wok over a medium–high heat and add the oil.
  Add the salmon and scallops and stir-fry for 3 minutes.
  Remove from the wok, set aside and keep warm.

2 Add the carrots, celery, peppers, mushrooms and garlic
  to the wok and stir-fry for 3 minutes. Add the coriander
  and shallots and stir.

3 Add the lime juice and zest, dried red pepper flakes,
  sherry and soy sauce and stir. Return the salmon and
  scallops to the wok and stir-fry carefully for another
  minute. Serve immediately.

spicy scallops with lime & chilli

ingredients

serves 4

16 large scallops, shelled
1 tbsp butter
1 tbsp vegetable oil
1 tsp crushed garlic
1 tsp grated fresh ginger
1 bunch of spring onions,
    finely sliced
finely grated rind of 1 lime
1 small fresh red chilli, deseeded
    and very finely chopped
3 tbsp lime juice
lime wedges, to garnish
freshly cooked rice, to serve

method

1 Using a sharp knife, trim the scallops to remove any black intestine, then wash and pat dry with kitchen paper. Separate the corals from the white parts, then slice each white part in half horizontally, making 2 circles.

2 Heat the butter and oil in a preheated wok. Add the garlic and ginger and stir-fry for 1 minute without browning. Add the spring onions and stir-fry for 1 minute.

3 Add the scallops and continue stir-frying over high heat for 4–5 minutes. Stir in the lime rind, chilli and lime juice and cook for a further 1 minute.

4 Transfer the scallops to serving plates, then spoon over the cooking juices and garnish with lime wedges. Serve hot with freshly cooked rice.

stir-fried scallops with asparagus

ingredients

serves 4

225 g/8 oz scallops
2 tsp salt
225 g/8 oz asparagus
3 tbsp vegetable or peanut oil
55 g/2 oz fresh or canned bamboo
  shoots, rinsed and thinly sliced
  (if using fresh shoots, boil in
  water first for 30 minutes)
1 small carrot, finely sliced
4 thin slices of fresh ginger
pinch of white pepper
2 tbsp Shaoxing rice wine
2 tbsp chicken stock
1 tsp sesame oil

method

1 Sprinkle the scallops with 1 teaspoon of the salt and set aside for 20 minutes.

2 Trim the asparagus, discarding the tough ends. Cut into 5-cm/2-inch pieces and blanch in a large pan of boiling water for 30 seconds. Drain and set aside.

3 In a preheated wok, heat 1 tablespoon of the oil and cook the scallops for 30 seconds. Drain and set aside.

4 In the clean wok, heat another tablespoon of the oil and stir-fry the asparagus, bamboo shoots and carrot for 2 minutes. Season with the remaining salt. Drain and set aside.

5 In the clean wok, heat the remaining oil, then add the ginger and stir-fry until fragrant. Return the scallops and vegetables to the wok and sprinkle with the pepper, Shaoxing and stock. Cover and continue cooking for 2 minutes, then toss through the sesame oil and serve.

scallops in black bean sauce

ingredients

serves 4

2 tbsp vegetable or peanut oil
1 tsp finely chopped garlic
1 tsp finely chopped
    fresh ginger
1 tbsp fermented black beans,
    rinsed and lightly mashed
400 g/14 oz scallops
½ tsp light soy sauce
1 tsp Shaoxing rice wine
1 tsp sugar
3–4 red Thai chillies, finely
    chopped
1–2 tsp chicken stock
1 tbsp finely chopped
    spring onion

method

1 In a preheated wok, heat the oil. Add the garlic and stir, then add the ginger and stir-fry together for about 1 minute, or until fragrant. Mix in the black beans, then toss in the scallops and stir-fry for 1 minute. Add the light soy sauce, Shaoxing, sugar and chillies.

2 Lower the heat and simmer for 2 minutes, adding the stock if necessary. Finally add the spring onion, then stir and serve.

sweet chilli squid

ingredients

serves 4

1 tbsp sesame seeds, toasted
2⅓ tbsp sesame oil
280 g/10 oz squid, cut into strips
2 red peppers, deseeded and
    thinly sliced
3 shallots, thinly sliced
85 g/3 oz mushrooms, thinly sliced
1 tbsp dry sherry
4 tbsp soy sauce
1 tsp sugar
1 tsp hot chilli flakes, or to taste
1 clove of garlic, crushed
freshly cooked plain rice, to serve

method

1 Place the sesame seeds on a baking sheet, toast under a hot grill and set aside.

2 Heat a wok over a medium heat and add 1 tablespoon of the oil. Add the squid and cook for 2 minutes, then remove and set aside.

3 Add another 1 tablespoon of the oil to the frying pan and fry the peppers and shallots over a medium heat for 1 minute. Add the mushrooms and fry for a further 2 minutes.

4 Return the squid to the frying pan and add the sherry, soy sauce, sugar, chilli flakes and garlic, stirring thoroughly. Cook for a further 2 minutes.

5 Sprinkle with the toasted sesame seeds, drizzle over the remaining sesame oil and mix. Serve on a bed of rice.

squid & red peppers

ingredients

serves 4

spice paste

2 tbsp vegetable or peanut oil
1 tbsp chilli oil with shrimp
2 shallots, chopped
2–3 large fresh red chillies,
    deseeded and chopped roughly
2 tbsp ground coriander
2 tbsp ground cumin
1-inch piece fresh ginger, chopped
1 tbsp finely chopped lemon grass
3–4 coriander roots, chopped
1 tsp salt
1 tsp jaggery or soft light
    brown sugar

stir-fry

2 red peppers, deseeded and diced
150 ml/5 fl oz plain yogurt
750 g/1 lb 10 oz squid, cleaned
    and sliced
juice of 1 lime
115 g/4 oz block creamed
    coconut, chopped
150 ml/5 fl oz hot water
freshly cooked rice, to serve

method

1 Put all the ingredients for the spice paste into a food processor and process until chopped finely.

2 Scrape the spice paste into a wok and stir-fry gently for 3–4 minutes. Add the red peppers and stir-fry for 1–2 minutes.

3 Add the yogurt and bring to the boil. Add the squid and simmer for 2–3 minutes, then stir in the lime juice, coconut and water. Simmer for a further 1–2 minutes, until the coconut dissolves. Serve immediately with freshly cooked rice.

prawns with spring onions & straw mushrooms

ingredients

serves 4

2 tbsp vegetable or peanut oil
bunch of spring onions, chopped
2 garlic cloves, chopped finely
175 g/6 oz block creamed
    coconut, chopped roughly
2 tbsp Thai red curry paste
450 ml/15 fl oz fish stock
2 tbsp fish sauce
2 tbsp Thai soy sauce
6 sprigs fresh Thai basil
400 g/14 oz canned straw
    mushrooms, drained
350 g/12 oz large cooked
    peeled prawns
boiled jasmine rice, to serve

method

1 Heat the oil in a wok and stir-fry the spring onions and garlic for 2–3 minutes. Add the creamed coconut, red curry paste and stock, and heat gently, stirring, until the coconut has dissolved.

2 Stir in the fish sauce and soy sauce, then add the basil, mushrooms and prawns. Gradually bring to the boil and serve at once with jasmine rice.

prawns fu yung

ingredients

serves 4–6

1 tbsp vegetable or peanut oil
115 g/4 oz raw prawns, peeled
    and deveined
4 eggs, lightly beaten
1 tsp salt
pinch of white pepper
2 tbsp finely chopped
    Chinese chives

method

1 In a preheated wok, heat the oil and stir-fry the prawns until they begin to turn pink.

2 Season the beaten eggs with the salt and pepper and pour over the prawns. Stir-fry for 1 minute, then add the chives.

3 Cook for a further 4 minutes, stirring all the time, until the eggs are cooked through but still soft in texture, and serve immediately.

wok-fried jumbo prawns in spicy sauce

ingredients

serves 4

3 tbsp vegetable or peanut oil
450 g/1 lb raw king prawns, deveined but unpeeled
2 tsp finely chopped fresh ginger
1 tsp finely chopped garlic
1 tbsp chopped spring onion
2 tbsp chilli bean sauce
1 tsp Shaoxing rice wine
1 tsp sugar
½ tsp light soy sauce
1–2 tbsp chicken stock

method

1 In a preheated wok, heat the oil, then toss in the prawns and stir-fry over high heat for about 4 minutes. Arrange the prawns on the sides of the wok out of the oil, then throw in the ginger and garlic and stir until fragrant. Add the spring onion and chilli bean sauce. Stir the prawns into this mixture.

2 Lower the heat slightly and add the Shaoxing, sugar, light soy sauce and a little chicken stock. Cover and cook for a further minute. Serve immediately.

tiger prawns in tamarind sauce

ingredients

serves 2

350 g raw headless tiger prawns, unshelled
1½ tbsp finely chopped fresh ginger
2 shallots, finely chopped
½ green chilli, deseeded and finely chopped
groundnut oil, for frying
3 tbsp chopped fresh coriander, to garnish
freshly cooked plain rice, to serve

tamarind sauce

1 tbsp tamarind paste
1 tbsp sugar
2 tsp oyster sauce
2 tbsp water
1 tsp fish sauce

method

1 Remove the shells from the prawns leaving the last segment and the tail in place. Combine the ginger, shallots and chilli in a small bowl. Combine the sauce ingredients in another bowl.

2 Heat a wok over a high heat, then add the oil. When the oil is almost smoking, add the prawns and stir-fry for 3–4 minutes until just pink. Remove from the wok and drain in a colander.

3 Pour off all but 2 tablespoons of oil from the wok. Heat the remaining oil over a high heat and stir-fry the ginger mixture for 1 minute. Add the tamarind sauce and stir for a few seconds until hot. Add the prawns and stir-fry for 1 minute until the sauce is slightly reduced.

4 Transfer the prawns to a warm serving dish and sprinkle with the coriander. Serve with rice.

clams in black bean sauce

ingredients

serves 4

900 g/2 lb small clams
1 tbsp vegetable or peanut oil
1 tsp finely chopped fresh
    ginger
1 tsp finely chopped garlic
1 tbsp fermented black beans,
    rinsed and roughly chopped
2 tsp Shaoxing rice wine
1 tbsp finely chopped spring onion
1 tsp salt (optional)

method

1 Start by washing the clams thoroughly, then soak
    them in clean water until it is time to drain them and
    toss them in the wok.

2 In a preheated wok, heat the oil and stir-fry the ginger
    and garlic until fragrant. Add the black beans and cook
    for 1 minute.

3 Over high heat, add the clams and Shaoxing and
    stir-fry for 2 minutes to mix everything together.
    Cover and cook for about 3 minutes. Add the spring
    onion and salt, if necessary, and serve immediately.

rice & noodles

egg-fried rice

ingredients

serves 4

2 tbsp vegetable or peanut oil
350 g/12 oz cooked rice, chilled
1 egg, well beaten

method

1 Heat the oil in a preheated wok and stir-fry the rice for 1 minute, breaking it down as much as possible into individual grains.

2 Quickly add the egg, stirring, so as to coat each piece of rice. Stir until the egg is cooked and the rice, as far as possible, is in single grains. Serve immediately.

egg-fried rice with vegetables & crispy onions

ingredients

serves 4

4 tbsp vegetable or peanut oil
2 garlic cloves, chopped finely
2 fresh red chillies, deseeded
    and chopped
115 g/4 oz mushrooms, sliced
55 g/2 oz mangetout, halved
55 g/2 oz baby corn cobs, halved
3 tbsp Thai soy sauce
1 tbsp jaggery or soft light
    brown sugar
few Thai basil leaves
350 g/12 oz rice, cooked
    and cooled
2 eggs, beaten
2 onions, sliced

method

1 Heat half the oil in a wok and sauté the garlic and chillies for 2–3 minutes.

2 Add the mushrooms, mangetout and corn and stir-fry for 2–3 minutes before adding the soy sauce, sugar and basil. Stir in the rice.

3 Push the mixture to one side of the wok and add the eggs to the bottom. Stir until lightly set before combining into the rice mixture.

4 Heat the remaining oil in another wok and sauté the onions until crispy and brown. Serve the rice topped with the onions.

egg fu yung

ingredients

serves 4–6

2 eggs
½ tsp salt
pinch of white pepper
1 tsp melted butter
2 tbsp vegetable or peanut oil
1 tsp finely chopped garlic
1 small onion, finely sliced
1 green pepper, finely sliced
450 g/1 lb cooked rice, chilled
1 tbsp light soy sauce
1 tbsp finely chopped spring onion
140 g/5 oz beansprouts, trimmed
2 drops of sesame oil

method

1 Beat the eggs with the salt and pepper. Heat the butter in a pan and pour in the eggs. Cook as an omelette, until set, then remove from the pan and cut into slivers.

2 In a preheated wok, heat the oil and stir-fry the garlic until fragrant. Add the onion and stir-fry for 1 minute, then add the green pepper and stir for 1 more minute. Stir in the rice and when the grains are separated, stir in the light soy sauce and cook for 1 minute.

3 Add the spring onion and egg strips and stir well, then finally add the beansprouts and sesame oil. Stir-fry for 1 minute and serve.

beef chow mein

ingredients

serves 4

280 g/10 oz tenderloin steak,
   cut into slivers
225 g/8 oz dried egg noodles
2 tbsp vegetable or peanut oil
1 onion, finely sliced
1 green pepper, finely sliced
140 g/5 oz beansprouts, trimmed
1 tsp salt
pinch of sugar
2 tsp Shaoxing rice wine
2 tbsp light soy sauce
1 tbsp dark soy sauce
1 tbsp finely shredded spring onion

marinade

1 tsp light soy sauce
dash of sesame oil
½ tsp Shaoxing rice wine
pinch of white pepper

method

1 Combine all the marinade ingredients in a bowl
   and marinate the beef for at least 20 minutes.

2 Cook the noodles according to the directions on
   the packet. When cooked, rinse under cold water and
   set aside.

3 In a preheated wok, heat the oil and stir-fry the beef
   for about 1 minute, or until the meat has changed
   colour, then add the onion and cook for 1 minute,
   followed by the pepper and beansprouts. Evaporate
   off any water from the vegetables. Add the salt, sugar,
   Shaoxing and soy sauces. Stir in the noodles and toss
   for 1 minute. Finally, stir in the spring onion and serve.

dan dan mian

ingredients

serves 4

1 tbsp vegetable or peanut oil
1 large dried chilli, deseeded and
   snipped into 3 pieces
½ tsp Sichuan peppers
100 g/3½ oz minced beef
2 tsp light soy sauce
300 g/10½ oz fine white noodles
1 tbsp roasted peanuts, chopped

sauce

1 tbsp preserved vegetables
½ tsp Sichuan peppers, lightly
   roasted and crushed
100 ml/3½ fl oz chicken stock
1 tsp black Chinese vinegar
1 tsp chilli oil
1 tsp dark soy sauce
1 tbsp light soy sauce
1 tbsp sesame paste
few drops of sesame oil
2 spring onions, finely chopped

method

1 Heat the oil in a preheated wok and toss in the chilli
   and peppers, then add the meat and stir rapidly. When
   the meat has changed colour, add the light soy sauce
   and continue to cook until the meat is well browned.
   Carefully mix the sauce ingredients together and pour
   into 4 noodle bowls.

2 Cook the noodles according to the directions on
   the packet. When cooked, drain and divide the noodles
   among the bowls.

3 Top with the meat mixture, then sprinkle with the roasted
   peanuts and serve at once. Mix well before eating.

fried rice
with pork & prawns

ingredients

serves 4

3 tsp vegetable or peanut oil
1 egg, lightly beaten
100 g/3½ oz raw prawns, peeled,
    deveined and cut into 2 pieces
100 g/3½ oz cha siu, finely
    chopped
2 tbsp finely chopped spring onion
200 g/7 oz cooked rice, chilled
1 tsp salt

method

1 In a preheated wok, heat 1 teaspoon of the oil and
  pour in the egg. Cook until scrambled. Remove and
  set aside.

2 Add the remaining oil and stir-fry the prawns, cha siu
  and spring onion for about 2 minutes. Add the rice
  and salt, breaking up the rice into grains, and cook for
  a further 2 minutes. Finally, stir in the cooked egg.
  Serve at once.

chicken fried rice

ingredients

serves 4

½ tbsp sesame oil
6 shallots, peeled and cut into
    quarters
450 g/1 lb cooked chicken, cubed
3 tbsp soy sauce
2 carrots, diced
1 celery stick, diced
1 red pepper, deseeded and diced
175 g/6 oz fresh peas
100 g/3½ oz canned sweetcorn,
    drained
275 g/9¾ oz cooked long-grain rice
2 large eggs, scrambled

method

1 Heat a wok over a medium heat, then add the oil.
   Add the shallots and cook until soft, then add the
   chicken and 2 tablespoons of the soy sauce and stir-fry
   for 5–6 minutes.

2 Stir in the carrots, celery, red pepper, peas and
   sweetcorn and stir-fry for a further 5 minutes. Add the
   rice and stir thoroughly.

3 Finally, stir in the scrambled eggs and the remaining
   soy sauce. Serve immediately.

variation

Replace the chicken with mushrooms or prawns to make
a tasty alternative.

pork lo mein

ingredients

serves 4–6

175 g/6 oz boneless lean
   pork, shredded
225 g/8 oz egg noodles
1½ tbsp vegetable or
   peanut oil
2 tsp finely chopped garlic
1 tsp finely chopped fresh ginger
1 carrot, julienned
225 g/8 oz finely sliced mushrooms
1 green pepper, thinly sliced
1 tsp salt
175 ml/6 fl oz hot chicken stock
200 g/7 oz beansprouts, trimmed
2 tbsp finely chopped spring onion

marinade

1 tsp light soy sauce
dash of sesame oil
pinch of white pepper

method

1 Combine all the marinade ingredients in a bowl
and marinate the pork for at least 20 minutes.

2 Cook the noodles according to the directions on
the packet. When cooked, drain and then set aside.

3 In a preheated wok, heat 1 teaspoon of the oil and
stir-fry the pork until the colour has changed. Remove
and set aside.

4 In the clean wok, heat the remaining oil and stir-fry
the garlic and ginger until fragrant. Add the carrot and
cook for 1 minute, then add the mushrooms and cook
for 1 minute. Toss in the pepper and cook for 1 minute.
Add the pork, salt and stock and heat through. Finally,
toss in the noodles, followed by the beansprouts, and
stir well. Sprinkle with the spring onion and serve.

rice with seafood & squid

ingredients

serves 4

2 tbsp vegetable or peanut oil

3 shallots, chopped finely

2 garlic cloves, chopped finely

225 g/8 oz jasmine rice

300 ml/10 fl oz fish stock

4 spring onions, chopped

2 tbsp Thai red curry paste

225 g/8 oz baby squid, cleaned
and sliced thickly

225 g/8 oz white fish fillets,
skinned and cut into cubes

225 g/8 oz salmon fillets, skinned
and cut into cubes

4 tbsp chopped fresh coriander

method

1 Heat 1 tablespoon of the oil in a wok and stir-fry the shallots and garlic for 2–3 minutes, until softened. Add the rice and stir-fry for 2–3 minutes.

2 Add a ladleful of the stock and simmer, adding more stock as needed, for 12–15 minutes, until tender. Transfer the stock to a dish and cool, then chill in the refrigerator overnight.

3 Heat the remaining oil in a wok and stir-fry the spring onions and curry paste for 2–3 minutes. Add the squid and fish and stir-fry gently to avoid breaking up the fish. Stir in the rice and coriander, heat through gently and serve.

beef with fresh noodles

ingredients

serves 4

6 dried black cloud Chinese
   mushrooms
2 tbsp vegetable or peanut oil
2 x 225-g/8-oz sirloin steaks,
   sliced thickly
1 onion, cut into thin wedges
2 garlic cloves, chopped
1 green pepper, deseeded
   and chopped
3 celery stalks, sliced
2 tbsp Thai green curry paste
300 ml/10 fl oz beef stock
4 tbsp black bean sauce
225 g/8 oz fresh egg noodles
4 tbsp chopped fresh parsley

method

1 Put the dried mushrooms in a bowl, cover with
   boiling water and soak for 30 minutes. Drain, then
   break up any larger pieces.

2 Heat the oil in a wok and stir-fry the steak over high
   heat until browned. Add the mushrooms, onion, garlic,
   pepper and celery and stir-fry for 3–4 minutes. Add the
   curry paste, beef stock and black bean sauce and
   stir-fry for 2–3 minutes.

3 Meanwhile, cook the noodles in boiling water for
   3–4 minutes, drain well and stir into the wok. Sprinkle
   the parsley over and stir. Serve immediately.

rice noodles with beef in black bean sauce

ingredients

serves 4–6

225 g/8 oz rump steak, finely sliced
225 g/8 oz rice sticks
2–3 tbsp vegetable or peanut oil
1 small onion, finely sliced
1 green pepper, finely sliced
1 red pepper, finely sliced
2 tbsp black bean sauce
2–3 tbsp light soy sauce

marinade

1 tbsp dark soy sauce
1 tsp Shaoxing rice wine
½ tsp sugar
½ tsp white pepper

method

1 Combine all the marinade ingredients in a bowl and marinate the beef for at least 20 minutes.

2 Cook the rice sticks according to the directions on the packet. When cooked, drain and set aside.

3 In a preheated wok, heat the oil and stir-fry the beef for 1 minute, or until the meat has changed colour. Drain the meat and set aside.

4 Pour off any excess oil from the wok and stir-fry the onion and peppers for 1 minute. Add the black bean sauce and stir well, then pour in the light soy sauce. Toss the rice sticks in the vegetables and, when fully incorporated, add the beef and stir until warmed through. Serve immediately.

sour & spicy pork

ingredients

serves 4

55 g/2 oz dried Chinese cloud
   ear mushrooms
100 g/3½ oz baby corn, halved
   lengthways
2 tbsp honey
1 tbsp tamarind paste
4 tbsp boiling water
2 tbsp dark soy sauce
1 tbsp rice vinegar
2 tbsp peanut or corn oil
1 large garlic clove, very
   finely chopped
1-cm/½-inch piece fresh ginger,
   peeled and very finely chopped
½ tsp dried red pepper flakes,
   or to taste
350 g/12 oz pork fillet,
   thinly sliced
4 spring onions, thickly sliced
   on the diagonal
1 green pepper, cored, deseeded
   and sliced
250 g/9 oz fresh Hokkien noodles
chopped fresh coriander,
   to garnish

method

1 Soak the mushrooms in enough boiling water to cover
   for 20 minutes, or until they are tender. Drain them
   well, then cut off and discard any thick stems, and slice
   the cups if they are large. Meanwhile, bring a large
   saucepan of lightly salted water to the boil, add the
   baby corn and blanch for 3 minutes. Drain the corn and
   run it under cold running water to stop the cooking,
   then set aside. Put the honey and tamarind paste in
   a small bowl and stir in the water, stirring until the
   paste dissolves. Stir in the soy sauce and rice vinegar
   and set aside.

2 Heat a wok over high heat. Add 1 tablespoon of the
   oil and heat until it shimmers. Add the garlic, ginger
   and red pepper flakes and stir-fry for about 30 seconds.
   Add the pork and continue stir-frying for 2 minutes.

3 Put the remaining oil in the wok and heat. Add the
   spring onions, pepper, mushrooms and baby corn,
   along with the tamarind mixture, and stir-fry for a
   further 2–3 minutes, until the pork is cooked through
   and the vegetables are tender, but still firm to the
   bite. Add the noodles and use 2 forks to mix all
   the ingredients together. When the noodles and
   sauce are hot, sprinkle with coriander.

pad thai

ingredients

serves 4

225 g/8 oz thick rice-stick noodles
2 tbsp vegetable or peanut oil
2 garlic cloves, chopped
2 fresh red chillies, deseeded
    and chopped
175 g/6 oz pork fillet,
    sliced thinly
115 g/4 oz uncooked prawns,
    peeled and chopped
8 fresh Chinese chives, chopped
2 tbsp fish sauce
juice of 1 lime
2 tsp jaggery or soft light
    brown sugar
2 eggs, beaten
115 g/4 oz beansprouts
4 tbsp chopped fresh coriander
115 g/4 oz unsalted peanuts,
    chopped, plus extra to serve
crispy fried onions, to serve

method

1 Soak the noodles in warm water for 10 minutes, drain well and set aside.

2 Heat the oil in a wok and stir-fry the garlic, chillies and pork for 2–3 minutes. Add the prawns to the wok and stir-fry for a further 2–3 minutes.

3 Add the chives and noodles, then cover and cook for 1–2 minutes. Add the fish sauce, lime juice, sugar and eggs. Cook, stirring and tossing constantly to mix in the eggs.

4 Stir in the beansprouts, coriander and peanuts, and serve with small dishes of crispy fried onions and extra chopped peanuts.

malaysian-style coconut noodles with prawns

ingredients

serves 4

2 tbsp vegetable oil
1 small red pepper, deseeded and diced
200 g/7 oz bok choi, stalks thinly sliced and leaves chopped
2 large garlic cloves, chopped
1 tsp ground turmeric
2 tsp garam masala
1 tsp chilli powder (optional)
125 ml/4 fl oz hot vegetable stock
2 heaped tbsp smooth peanut butter
350 ml/12 fl oz coconut milk
1 tbsp soy sauce
250 g/9 oz thick rice noodles
280 g/10 oz cooked peeled jumbo prawns
2 spring onions, finely shredded and 1 tbsp sesame seeds, to garnish

method

1 Heat a wok over a high heat and add the oil. Add the red pepper, bok choi stalks and garlic and stir-fry for 3 minutes. Add the turmeric, garam masala, chilli powder, if using, and bok choi leaves and stir-fry for 1 minute.

2 Mix the hot stock and peanut butter together in a heatproof bowl until the peanut butter has dissolved, then add to the stir-fry with the coconut milk and soy sauce. Cook for 5 minutes over a medium heat, or until reduced and thickened.

3 Soak the noodles in enough lukewarm water to cover for 15 minutes, or cook according to the instructions on the packet, until soft. Drain and refresh the noodles under cold running water. Add the cooked noodles and prawns to the coconut curry and cook for a further 2–3 minutes, stirring frequently, until heated through.

4 Serve the noodle dish sprinkled with spring onions and sesame seeds.

teriyaki chicken with sesame noodles

ingredients

serves 4

4 boneless chicken breasts, about
    175 g/6 oz each, with or
    without skin, as you wish
about 4 tbsp bottled teriyaki sauce
peanut or corn oil

sesame noodles

250 g/9 oz dried thin buckwheat
    noodles
1 tbsp toasted sesame oil
2 tbsp toasted sesame seeds
2 tbsp finely chopped fresh parsley
salt and pepper

method

1 Using a sharp knife, score each chicken breast diagonally across 3 times and rub all over with teriyaki sauce. Set aside to marinate for at least 10 minutes, or cover and chill all day.

2 When you are ready to cook the chicken, preheat the grill to high. Bring a saucepan of water to the boil, add the buckwheat noodles and boil for 3 minutes, until soft. Alternatively, cook according to the packet instructions. Drain and rinse well in cold water to stop the cooking and remove excess starch, then drain again.

3 Lightly brush the grill rack with oil. Add the chicken breasts, skin side up, and brush again with a little extra teriyaki sauce. Grill the chicken breasts about 10 cm/4 inches from the heat, brushing occasionally with extra teriyaki sauce, for 15 minutes, or until cooked through and the juices run clear.

4 Meanwhile, heat a wok over high heat. Add the sesame oil and heat until it shimmers. Add the noodles and stir round to heat through, then stir in the sesame seeds and parsley. Finally, add salt and pepper to taste.

5 Transfer the chicken breasts to plates and add a portion of noodles to each.

yaki soba

ingredients

serves 2

400 g/14 oz ramen noodles
1 onion, finely sliced
200 g/7 oz beansprouts
1 red pepper, dedeseeded and
   finely shredded
1 boneless, skin-on cooked chicken
   breast, about 150 g/5½ oz,
   cooked and sliced
12 cooked peeled prawns
1 tbsp oil
2 tbsp shoyu (Japanese soy sauce)
½ tbsp mirin
1 tsp sesame oil
1 tsp roasted sesame seeds
2 spring onions, finely sliced

method

1 Cook the noodles according to the packet instructions, drain well, and tip into a bowl.

2 Mix the onion, beansprouts, red pepper, chicken and prawns together in a separate bowl. Stir through the noodles.

3 Preheat a wok over high heat. Add the oil and heat until very hot. Add the noodle mixture and stir-fry for 4 minutes, or until golden, then add the shoyu, mirin and sesame oil and toss together.

4 Divide the mixture between 2 plates, sprinkle with the sesame seeds and spring onions and serve at once.

vegetarian

aubergine with red peppers

ingredients

serves 4

3 tbsp vegetable or peanut oil
1 garlic clove, finely chopped
3 aubergines, halved lengthways
   and cut diagonally into
   2.5-cm/1-inch pieces
1 tsp white rice vinegar
1 red pepper, finely sliced
2 tbsp light soy sauce
1 tsp sugar
1 tbsp finely chopped coriander
   leaves, to garnish

method

1 In a preheated wok, heat the oil. When it begins to smoke, toss in the garlic and stir-fry until fragrant, then add the aubergine pieces. Stir-fry for 30 seconds, then add the vinegar. Turn down the heat and cook, covered, for 5 minutes, stirring occasionally.

2 When the aubergine pieces are soft, add the pepper and stir. Add the light soy sauce and sugar and cook, uncovered, for 2 minutes.

3 Remove from the heat and stand for 2 minutes. Transfer to a dish, then garnish with chopped coriander and serve.

aubergine stir-fry with hot & sour sauce

ingredients

serves 4

150 ml/5 fl oz vegetable stock

2 aubergines, peeled

6 tbsp groundnut oil

2 red peppers, deseeded and cut into matchstick strips

100 g/3½ oz canned drained water chestnuts, sliced

6 spring onions, sliced

2 tsp finely chopped fresh ginger

1 large garlic clove, thinly sliced

1 green chilli, deseeded and finely chopped

salt and pepper

1 tsp sesame seeds and thinly sliced spring onion tops, to garnish

freshly cooked plain rice, to serve

sauce

1½ tbsp soy sauce

1½ tbsp rice vinegar

2 tsp sugar

2 tsp cornflour, blended to a smooth paste with a little water

method

1 First prepare the sauce. Combine the soy sauce, rice vinegar and sugar in a small bowl, stirring to dissolve the sugar. Mix in the cornflour paste and stir until smooth.

2 Heat the stock and set aside.

3 Slice the aubergines in half lengthways. With the flat side facing down, slice each half lengthways into 1-cm/¼-inch strips. Slice the wider strips lengthways in half again, then cut all the strips crossways into 4-cm/1¼-inch pieces.

4 Heat a wok over a high heat and add 5 tablespoons of the oil. Add the aubergine and red pepper strips and stir-fry for 2–3 minutes until just beginning to colour. Remove from the wok and drain on kitchen paper.

5 Heat the remaining tablespoon of oil over a high heat. Stir-fry the water chestnuts, spring onions, ginger, garlic and chilli for 1 minute.

6 Return the aubergine and red pepper to the wok. Reduce the heat to medium, and add soy sauce and the stock. Stir-fry for 2–3 minutes until slightly thickened. Sprinkle with sesame seeds and sliced spring onion tops. Serve with rice.

aubergine with miso

ingredients

serves 4

2 aubergines
oil, for stir-frying
1 fresh red chilli, sliced
2 tbsp sake
4 tbsp mirin
2 tbsp shoyu (Japanese soy sauce)
3 tbsp hatcho miso
2 tbsp water

method

1 Cut the aubergines into wedges.

2 Preheat a wok over high heat. Add a little oil and heat until very hot. Stir-fry the aubergine, in batches, for 4 minutes, or until browned and cooked through.

3 Return all the aubergine to the wok together with the chilli and stir together. Add the remaining ingredients and toss everything together. Cook, stirring, until the sauce thickens. Serve immediately.

hot & sour courgettes

ingredients

serves 4

2 large courgettes, thinly sliced
1 tsp salt
2 tbsp groundnut oil
1 tsp Sichuan pepper, crushed
½–1 red chilli, deseeded and
    sliced into thin strips
1 large garlic clove, thinly sliced
½ tsp finely chopped fresh ginger
1 tbsp rice vinegar
1 tbsp light soy sauce
2 tsp sugar
1 spring onion, green part
    included, thinly sliced
a few drops of sesame oil,
    to garnish
1 tsp sesame seeds, to garnish

method

1 Put the courgette slices in a large colander and toss with the salt. Cover with a plate and put a weight on top. Leave to drain for 20 minutes. Rinse off the salt and spread out the slices on kitchen paper to dry.

2 Heat a wok over a high heat and add the groundnut oil. Add the Sichuan pepper, chilli, garlic and ginger. Fry for about 20 seconds until the garlic is just beginning to colour.

3 Add the courgette slices and toss in the oil. Add the rice vinegar, soy sauce and sugar, and stir-fry for 2 minutes. Add the spring onion and fry for 30 seconds. Sprinkle with the sesame oil and seeds, and serve immediately.

broccoli with peanuts

ingredients

serves 4

3 tbsp vegetable or groundnut oil
1 lemon grass stem, roughly
    chopped
2 fresh red chillies, deseeded
    and chopped
2.5-cm/1-inch piece fresh ginger,
    grated
3 kaffir lime leaves, roughly torn
3 tbsp Thai green curry paste
1 onion, chopped
1 red pepper, deseeded
    and chopped
350 g/12 oz broccoli,
    cut into florets
115 g/4 oz French beans
55 g/2 oz unsalted peanuts

method

1 Put 2 tablespoons of the oil, the lemon grass, chillies, ginger, lime leaves and curry paste into a food processor or blender and process to a paste.

2 Heat a wok over a medium heat and add the remaining oil. Add the spice paste, onion and red pepper and stir-fry for 2–3 minutes, until the vegetables start to soften.

3 Add the broccoli and French beans, cover and cook over a low heat, stirring occasionally, for 4–5 minutes, until tender.

4 Meanwhile, toast or dry-fry the peanuts until lightly browned. Add them to the broccoli mixture and toss together. Serve immediately.

mixed vegetables with quick-fried basil

ingredients

serves 4

2 tbsp vegetable or peanut oil

2 garlic cloves, chopped

1 onion, sliced

115 g/4 oz baby corn cobs, cut in half diagonally

½ cucumber, peeled, halved, deseeded and sliced

225 g/8 oz canned water chestnuts, drained and rinsed

55 g/2 oz mangetout, trimmed

115 g/4 oz shiitake mushrooms, halved

1 red pepper, deseeded and sliced thinly

1 tbsp jaggery or soft light brown sugar

2 tbsp Thai soy sauce

1 tbsp fish sauce

1 tbsp rice vinegar

boiled rice, to serve

quick-fried basil

vegetable or peanut oil, for cooking

8–12 sprigs fresh Thai basil

method

1 Heat the oil in a wok and stir-fry the garlic and onion for 1–2 minutes. Add the corn cobs, cucumber, water chestnuts, mangetout, mushrooms and red pepper and stir-fry for 2–3 minutes, until starting to soften.

2 Add the sugar, soy sauce, fish sauce and vinegar and gradually bring to the boil. Simmer for 1–2 minutes.

3 Meanwhile, heat the oil for the basil in a wok and, when hot, add the basil sprigs. Cook for 20–30 seconds, until crisp. Remove with a slotted spoon and drain on kitchen paper.

4 Garnish the vegetable stir-fry with the crispy basil and serve immediately, with the boiled rice.

sweet-&-sour vegetables with cashew nuts

ingredients

serves 4

1 tbsp vegetable or peanut oil
1 tsp chilli oil
2 onions, sliced
2 carrots, sliced thinly
2 courgettes, sliced thinly
115 g/4 oz head of broccoli,
    cut into florets
115 g/4 oz white mushrooms,
    sliced
115 g/4 oz small pak choi, halved
2 tbsp jaggery or soft light
    brown sugar
2 tbsp Thai soy sauce
1 tbsp rice vinegar
55 g/2 oz cashew nuts

method

1 Heat the vegetable or peanut oil and the chilli oil in a wok and stir-fry the onions for 1–2 minutes, until they start to soften.

2 Add the carrots, courgettes and broccoli, and stir-fry for 2–3 minutes. Add the mushrooms, pak choi, sugar, soy sauce and rice vinegar and stir-fry for 1–2 minutes.

3 Meanwhile, dry-fry or toast the cashew nuts. Sprinkle the cashews over the stir-fry and serve immediately.

hot-&-sour cabbage

ingredients

serves 4

450 g/1 lb firm white cabbage
1 tbsp vegetable or peanut oil
10 Sichuan peppers or more,
    to taste
3 dried chillies, roughly chopped
½ tsp salt
1 tsp white rice vinegar
dash of sesame oil
pinch of sugar

method

1 To prepare the cabbage, discard the outer leaves and tough stems. Chop the cabbage into 3-cm/1¼-inch squares, breaking up the chunks. Rinse thoroughly in cold water.

2 In a preheated wok, heat the oil and cook the peppers until fragrant. Stir in the chillies. Throw in the cabbage, a little at a time, together with the salt and stir-fry for 2 minutes.

3 Add the vinegar, sesame oil and sugar and cook for a further minute, or until the cabbage is tender. Serve immediately.

spicy green beans

ingredients

serves 4

200 g/7 oz green beans, trimmed
and cut diagonally into
3–4 pieces
2 tbsp vegetable or peanut oil
4 dried chillies, cut into
2 or 3 pieces
½ tsp Sichuan peppers
1 garlic clove, finely sliced
6 thin slices of fresh ginger
2 spring onions, white part only,
cut diagonally into thin pieces
pinch of sea salt

method

1 Blanch the beans in a large pan of boiling water
for 30 seconds. Drain and set aside.

2 In a preheated wok, heat 1 tablespoon of the oil. Over
low heat, stir-fry the beans for about 5 minutes, or until
they are beginning to wrinkle. Remove and set aside.

3 Add the remaining oil and stir-fry the chillies and
peppers until they are fragrant. Add the garlic, ginger
and spring onions and stir-fry until they begin to
soften. Throw in the beans and toss to mix, then add
the sea salt and serve immediately.

julienne vegetable salad

ingredients

serves 4

4 tbsp vegetable or peanut oil
225 g/8 oz tofu with herbs, cubed
1 red onion, sliced
4 spring onions, cut into
    5-cm/2-inch lengths
1 garlic clove, chopped
2 carrots, cut into short, thin sticks
115 g/4 oz fine green beans, trimmed
1 yellow pepper, deseeded and
    cut into strips
115 g/4 oz head of broccoli,
    cut into florets
1 large courgette, cut into short,
    thin sticks
55 g/2 oz beansprouts
2 tbsp Thai red curry paste
4 tbsp Thai soy sauce
1 tbsp rice wine vinegar
1 tsp jaggery or soft light
    brown sugar
few Thai basil leaves
350 g/12 oz rice vermicelli noodles

method

1 Heat the oil in a wok and cook the tofu cubes for
   3–4 minutes, until browned on all sides. Lift the cubes
   out of the oil and drain on kitchen paper.

2 Add the onions, garlic and carrots to the hot oil and
   cook for 1–2 minutes before adding the rest of the
   vegetables, except for the beansprouts. Stir-fry for
   2–3 minutes. Add the beansprouts, then stir in the
   curry paste, soy, vinegar, sugar and basil leaves.
   Cook for 30 seconds.

3 Soak the noodles in boiling water or stock for
   2–3 minutes (check the packet instructions) or until
   tender and drain well.

4 Pile the vegetables onto the noodles, and serve topped
   with the tofu cubes. Garnish with extra basil if desired.

broccoli & mangetout stir-fry

ingredients

serves 4

2 tbsp vegetable or peanut oil
dash of sesame oil
1 garlic clove, finely chopped
225 g/8 oz small head of
    broccoli florets
115 g/4 oz mangetout, trimmed
225 g/8 oz Chinese leaves,
    chopped into 1-cm/
    ½-inch slices
5–6 spring onions, finely chopped
½ tsp salt
2 tbsp light soy sauce
1 tbsp Shaoxing rice wine
1 tsp sesame seeds, lightly toasted

method

1 In a preheated wok, heat the oils, then add the garlic and stir-fry vigorously. Add all the vegetables and salt and stir-fry over high heat, tossing rapidly, for about 3 minutes.

2 Pour in the light soy sauce and Shaoxing and cook for a further 2 minutes. Sprinkle with the sesame seeds and serve hot.

stir-fried long beans with red pepper

ingredients

serves 4–6

280 g/10 oz long beans, cut into
    6-cm/2½-inch lengths
1 tbsp vegetable or peanut oil
1 red pepper, slivered
pinch of salt
pinch of sugar

method

1 Blanch the beans in a large pan of boiling water for
   30 seconds. Drain and set aside.

2 In a preheated wok, heat the oil and stir-fry the beans
   for 1 minute over high heat. Add the pepper and
   stir-fry for 1 more minute. Sprinkle the salt and sugar
   on top and serve.

variation

You can add as many different vegetables as you like to
this recipe – green peppers and mangetout would go
well, as would carrots and mushrooms.

stir-fried chinese greens

ingredients

serves 4

1 tbsp vegetable or peanut oil
1 tsp finely chopped garlic
225 g/8 oz leafy Chinese leaves,
    roughly chopped
½ tsp salt

method

1 In a preheated wok, heat the oil and stir-fry the garlic
   until fragrant. Over high heat, toss in the Chinese leaves
   and salt and stir-fry for 1 minute maximum.

2 Serve immediately.

stir-fried beansprouts

ingredients

serves 4

1 tbsp vegetable or peanut oil
225 g/8 oz beansprouts, trimmed
2 tbsp finely chopped spring onion
½ tsp salt
pinch of sugar

method

1 In a preheated wok, heat the oil and stir-fry the beansprouts with the spring onion for about 1 minute. Add the salt and sugar and stir.

2 Serve immediately.

aubergine & bean curry

ingredients

serves 4

2 tbsp vegetable or peanut oil
1 onion, chopped
2 garlic cloves, crushed
2 fresh red chillies, deseeded and
   chopped
1 tbsp Thai red curry paste
1 large aubergine, cut into
   chunks
115 g/4 oz pea or small aubergines
115 g/4 oz baby broad beans
115 g/4 oz fine green beans
300 ml/10 fl oz vegetable stock
55 g/2 oz block creamed
   coconut, chopped
3 tbsp Thai soy sauce
1 tsp jaggery or soft light
   brown sugar
3 kaffir lime leaves, torn coarsely
4 tbsp chopped fresh coriander

method

1 Heat the oil in a wok and sauté the onion, garlic and
   chillies for 1–2 minutes. Stir in the curry paste and cook
   for 1–2 minutes.

2 Add the aubergines and cook for 3–4 minutes, until
   starting to soften. (You may need to add a little more
   oil as aubergines soak it up quickly.) Add all the beans
   and stir-fry for 2 minutes.

3 Pour in the stock and add the creamed coconut, soy
   sauce, sugar and lime leaves. Bring gently to the boil
   and cook until the coconut has dissolved. Stir in the
   coriander and serve hot.

tofu & green vegetable curry

ingredients

serves 4

vegetable or peanut oil,
  for deep-frying
225 g/8 oz firm tofu, cut into cubes
2 tbsp vegetable or peanut oil
1 tbsp chilli oil
2 fresh green chillies, deseeded
  and sliced
2 garlic cloves, crushed
6 spring onions, sliced
2 medium courgettes,
  cut into sticks
½ cucumber, peeled, deseeded
  and sliced
1 green pepper, deseeded
  and sliced
1 small head of broccoli,
  cut into florets
55 g/2 oz fine green beans, halved
55 g/2 oz frozen peas, thawed
300 ml/10 fl oz vegetable stock
55 g/2 oz block creamed coconut,
  chopped
2 tbsp Thai soy sauce
1 tsp soft light brown sugar
4 tbsp chopped fresh parsley,
  to garnish

method

1 Heat the oil for deep-frying in a wok and carefully lower in the tofu cubes, in batches, and cook for 2–3 minutes, until golden brown. Remove with a slotted spoon and drain on kitchen paper.

2 Heat the other oils in a wok and stir-fry the chillies, garlic and spring onions for 2–3 minutes. Add the courgettes, cucumber, green pepper, broccoli and green beans, and stir-fry for a further 2–3 minutes.

3 Add the peas, stock, coconut, soy sauce and sugar. Cover and simmer for 2–3 minutes, until all the vegetables are tender and the coconut has dissolved.

4 Stir in the tofu and serve immediately, sprinkled with the parsley.

spicy tofu with rice

ingredients

serves 6

250 g/9 oz firm tofu, rinsed, drained
and cut into 1-cm/½-inch cubes
4 tbsp groundnut oil
1 tbsp grated fresh ginger
3 garlic cloves, crushed
4 spring onions, thinly sliced
1 head of broccoli, cut into florets
1 carrot, cut into batons
1 yellow pepper, deseeded and
thinly sliced
250 g/9 oz shiitake mushrooms,
thinly sliced
freshly cooked plain rice, to serve

marinade

5 tbsp vegetable stock
2 tsp cornflour
2 tbsp light soy sauce
1 tbsp caster sugar
pinch of chilli flakes

method

1 Combine all the marinade ingredients in a bowl.
Add the tofu and toss well to cover in the marinade.
Set aside to marinate for 20 minutes.

2 Heat a wok over a medium–high heat and add
2 tablespoons of the oil. Stir-fry the tofu with its
marinade until brown and crispy. Remove from
the wok and set aside.

3 Heat the remaining 2 tablespoons of oil in the wok
and stir-fry the ginger, garlic and spring onions for
30 seconds. Add the broccoli, carrot, yellow pepper
and mushrooms and cook for 5–6 minutes. Return
the tofu to the wok and stir-fry to reheat. Serve
immediately with rice.

agedashi tofu

ingredients

serves 2

150 ml/5 fl oz water
2 tsp dashi granules
2 tbsp shoyu (Japanese
    soy sauce)
2 tbsp mirin
vegetable oil, for deep-frying
300 g/10½ oz silken tofu,
    drained on kitchen paper and
    cut into 4 cubes
2 tbsp plain flour
1 tsp grated fresh ginger
2 tsp grated daikon
¼ tsp kezuri-bushi shavings

method

1 Put the water in a pan with the dashi granules and bring to the boil. Add the shoyu and mirin and cook for 1 minute. Keep warm.

2 Preheat a wok, then fill one-third full with oil, or use a deep-fryer. Heat the oil to 180–190°C/350–375°F, or until a cube of bread browns in 30 seconds. Meanwhile, dust the tofu cubes with the flour.

3 Add the tofu pieces to the oil, in batches, and cook until lightly golden in colour. Remove, drain on kitchen paper and keep hot while you cook the remaining tofu cubes.

4 Put 2 pieces of tofu in each of 2 bowls and divide the dashi stock between them. Top with ginger, daikon and kezuri-bushi.

index

agedashi tofu 206
aubergine
  aubergine & bean curry 200
  aubergine stir-fry with hot & sour sauce 174
  aubergine with miso 176
  aubergine with red peppers 172

beef
  beef chop suey 54
  beef chow mein 144
  beef stir-fry 24
  beef with mushrooms & fresh noodles 156
  beef with onions & broccoli 52
  spicy beef & mushroom wontons 20
  spicy beef with potato 56
  stir-fried beef with broccoli & ginger 58
  broccoli with peanuts 180

chicken
  chicken fried rice 150
  chicken noodle soup 10
  chicken with cashew nuts 76
  chicken with yellow curry sauce 86
  ginger chicken with sesame seeds 84
  gong bau chicken 80
  kara-age chicken 18
  peppered chicken stir-fry 82
  red chicken salad 88
  sweet-&-sour chicken 78
  teriyaki chicken with sesame noodles 166
clams in black bean sauce 134
crab parcels 38
crispy dishes
  crispy pork dumplings 26
  crispy seaweed 46
  crisp sesame prawns 36
  crispy wrapped prawns 32

dan dan mian 146
duck
  Cantonese sweet & sour duck 98
  duck with mixed peppers 96
  duck with spring onion soup 14
  fruity duck stir-fry 94

egg fu yung 142

fish and seafood
  clams in black bean sauce 134
  crab parcels 38
  fish curry 108
  fish in coconut 102
  five-willow fish 104
  mixed seafood curry 110
  monkfish with lime & chilli sauce 106
  salmon & scallops with coriander & lime 114
  scallops in black bean sauce 120
  spicy scallops with lime & chilli 116
  squid & red peppers 124
  steamed salmon with bok choi & aparagus 112
  stir-fried scallops with asparagus 118
  sweet chilli squid 122

ginger chicken with sesame seeds 84

hot & sour corgettes 178
hot & sour cabbage 186

julienne vegetable salad 190

kara-age chicken 18
katsudon 62

lamb
  fried lamb balls with spicy onion sauce 22
  lamb & leek stir-fry 74

ma po doufu 60
mushroom & noodle soup 8

noodles
  Malaysian-style coconut noodles with prawns 164
  beef with fresh noodles 156
  rice noodles with beef in black bean sauce 158

pad Thai 162
pork
  hot & sour pork soup with bamboo shoots 16
  pork, carrot & ginger stir-fry 66
  pork lo mein 152
  pork stir-fry with cashews, lime & mint 64
  pork with peppers 70
  sour & spicy pork 160
  spicy Sichuan pork 68
prawns
  crisp sesame prawns 36
  prawn toasts 34
  prawns fu yung 128
  prawns with spring onions & straw mushrooms 126
  tiger prawns in tamarind sauce 132
  wok-fried jumbo prawns in spicy sauce 130

rice
  chicken fried-rice 150
  egg-fried rice 138
  egg-fried rice with vegetables & crispy onions 140
  fried rice with pork & prawns 148
  rice with seafood & squid 154

soft-wrapped pork & prawn rolls 28
spareribs in a sweet-&-sour sauce 72
spicy green beans 188
spicy tofu with rice 204
spring rolls 30
steamed salmon with bok choi & aparagus 112
stir-fried dishes
  broccoli & mangetout stir-fry 192
  stir-fried beansprouts 198
  stir-fried Chinese greens 196
  stir-fried long beans with red pepper 194
  sweet-&-sour vegetables with cashew nuts 184

tempura 48
Thai-style seafood soup 12
tiger prawns in tamarind sauce 132
tofu & green vegetable curry 202
turkey
  turkey teriyaki 90
  turkey with bok choi & mushrooms 92

vegetable
  mixed vegetables with quick-fried basil 182
  vegetable parcels 42
  vegetarian spring rolls 40

wontons 44

yaki soba 168